Please return/renew this item by the last date shown.
Items may also be renewed by the internet*

https://library.eastriding.gov.uk

* Please note a PIN will be required to access this service
- this can be obtained from your library

D0833934

902856054 8

HOLD THE FRONT PAGE!

HOLD THE FRONT PAGE!

The Wit and Wisdom of Anne Scott-James

Clare Hastings

PIMPERNEL
PRESS LTD
www.pimpernelpress.com

Pimpernel Press Limited
www.pimpernelpress.com

Hold the Front Page!
The Wit and Wisdom of Anne Scott-James
© Pimpernel Press Limited 2020
Text by Clare Hastings
© Clare Hastings 2020
Articles by Anne Scott-James by kind
permission *Daily Express*/Express
Syndication
For copyright in the photographs
see page 208.
Design by Becky Clarke Design

A catalogue record for this book is
available from the British Library.

ISBN 978-1-910258-71-2

Typeset in American Typewriter and
Clarendon LT
Printed and bound in China
by C&C Offset Printing Company Limited

9 8 7 6 5 4 3 2 1

FRONT COVER Iconic shot of Anne for *Picture Post*, 1941.
PAGE 2 Anne when she joined the staff as Woman's Editor at *Picture Post*, 1941.

CONTENTS

I get words all day through.
First from him, now from you!
Is that all you blighters can do?'

Eliza Doolittle, *My Fair Lady*

Why write about Anne?

Presented with a blank page, my family would not hesitate to fill it.

Grandparents, parents, my brother, stepfather, writers all. They seem and seemed never happier than when committing words to a page. Plays, detective stories, military history, gardening, children's stories, a cookbook, interviews and opinions, the words flowed.

I have bookshelves at home that testify to their output, good, bad and brilliant – and sometimes irritatingly translated into different languages – talking up much-needed shelf space.

I haven't quite reached the stage where I can just box up the spares and send them to the great recycler. Parting with words, even when I can't actually read them, gives me a moment of unease. They can be useful too. A gardening book of my mother's in Japanese proved an inspired gift on a tour of Tokyo, and a tome of my brother's in Swedish went down a storm with a friend from Malmö.

It seems not only natural but inevitable that eventually I too should add to the weight on the shelf, stop faffing about on the sidelines and join in with the scribblers.

This book is written as a tribute to my mother, the writer Anne Scott-James, and in particular to her skills as a journalist. She perfected the art of writing the short, sharp style of column so familiar today. Leading the way for Katharine Whitehorn, Ann Leslie, Lynda Lee-Potter, Jill Tweedie and the raft of opinionated women journalists that followed her.

My mother died on 13 May 2009, and although I have an archive of her work, I have not spent much time reading it. Goodness, I lived through most of it. However, in the last couple of years, I have started to receive emails from writers keen to discover more about her. The woman who left university after only two years, to devote a lifetime to print. They often apply the metaphor – which Anne herself would have found deeply irritating – of 'breaking the glass ceiling'. She certainly did not see herself as forging a path for other women. Quite enough to forge her own. She was a journalist who happened to be a woman. She knew her column was not cerebral or reflective, but it was an excellent form of self-expression.

Anne thought about all her writing as having the potential to be published. She kept letters between herself and my stepfather, cartoonist Osbert Lancaster, labelled 'not to be published until six years after my death'; she also wrote to him every day for the year after he died, just keeping him up to speed with events and her feelings (especially about bereavement). These, again, are labelled with a publishing time frame. Anne was a professional writer, who knew her worth, and expected her words to find an audience.

It was while I was dealing with one of these requests for publication rights that it suddenly seemed obvious to me, that I, who knew her best, should be the one to offer an opinion of her. Although I was a child when she first embraced journalism and the world of Fleet Street – simply 'there', you could say – I think the 'there' is quite important. I can say, with hand on heart, that I know, or could hazard a pretty good guess at, her response to most events and situations. Any writer with a half-decent researcher can track her writing path, but no one will have spent a fraction of the time I have studying their subject. It is with this in mind that I am now offering my very personal take on Anne Scott-James. My mother was always very crisp about biographers who failed to interview relevant friends and acquaintances in a timely fashion: 'They'll all be dead before he gets round to them.' Biographers, apparently, not being renowned for moving at a swift pace. This remark, as with so many of Anne's, is at the forefront of my mind as I, too, inevitably grow older.

The key to understanding my mother is to read her pieces. Anne worked as woman's editor for *Picture Post*, before moving to become editor of *Harper's Bazaar*. After becoming pregnant (with me), she 'retired' from day-to-day editing and kept her hand in by writing the novel *In the Mink*, a thinly disguised autobiography, essentially a book about her. But I have decided to concentrate on the period of her life when she was at her happiest in work, when she first stepped on to the paving stones of Fleet Street to begin working for the *Sunday Express*. She wrote 'The Anne Scott-James Page' for that paper from 1953 to 1957. There followed a period of two years when, less happily, she wrote her page first for the *Sunday Dispatch* and then for the *Daily Express*. In 1960 she 'crossed the street', leaving the *Express* to write for the *Daily Mail*.

Her *Express* articles remain, nearly seventy years later, fresh, witty, and above all a pleasure to read. They are reproduced here as they appeared in the paper. I have not included many pieces on fashion, although they are entertaining. 'Fashion Trailer of the Week', 'Are You Always a Year Too Late?', 'Now Here Comes the Scooter-Girl' are headlines that could grip anyone with even a mild interest in period fashion; but when you get down to the minutiae of sashes, swimwear and shoes, they seem best left to one side, as they do not reveal very much about the person. I could have put in some of her longer pieces – often a whole page could be dedicated to one subject – but the articles shown here are to give you a flavour of Anne and the range of topics she covered.

Anne is probably at this point experiencing a moment of slight unease. My last attempt to reveal the happy home life of the Scott-James household was at the age of fourteen. I was interviewed for a piece on mothers and daughters for a magazine called *Honey*, aimed at the 'Young, Gay and Get-Ahead'. I was one of five girls asked to give forth on their mothers. Not a success, I'm afraid. Apparently the journalist was appalled that any child could say such terrible things about a parent. My mother, after a tricky conversation with the editor, allowed the piece to be included, managing to secure a promise that my surname was removed. The article showed the interviewee as Miss Clare X. It led my brother to advise me 'not to come home', and me to deny any truth in the article at all, claiming 'judicial editing' as the culprit. In my defence, the journalist *was* very soothing and the hour spent in her company had been most comforting, as, funnily enough, she had shown a rare and flattering interest in my feelings and teenage angst.

Anyway, I hope to do better this time round . . .

Anne Scott-James Timeline 1913–2009

Born 5 April 1913, in Bayswater, London

From the age of four and a half to ten attends Norland Place School, Holland Park, London.

From the age of ten to eighteen is at St Paul's Girls' School, Hammersmith, London.

Throughout her childhood lives in Bayswater. Her father is lead writer for the *Daily Chronicle*, then Literary Editor of the *Daily News*. Mother writes a weekly 'letter' for the *Yorkshire Post*. Her older sister, Marie, is a literary critic for *The Observer*.

1931–2 Somerville College Oxford. Goes up on a scholarship to read Classics. Gains a First in Honour Moderations ('Mods'), but leaves at the end of her second year to start work.

1933 Writes for *Weldon's* magazine, answering readers' letters.

1933 Works at Harrods, selling in the Christmas Toys department.

1934 Job on *Vogue*, working for the knitting pattern editor. Stays at *Vogue* for seven years, during which time she moves to the editorial department and later becomes Beauty Editor.

1936 Moves from home to rented flat on King's Road, Chelsea, London.

1938 Buys Rose Cottage, Oxfordshire, at auction, This cottage was to influence her life. At this time, and for long after, her London homes were always rented: Rutland Gate, Queensway, Cromwell Road.

1939 Marries Derek Verschoyle, publisher and editor of *The Spectator*. Marriage lasts a few months.

1940 Applies to *Picture Post* to write a story on *Vogue*.

1941 Offered job as woman's editor on *Picture Post*, works on the magazine through the war years.

1944. Marries Macdonald Hastings, journalist and broadcaster.

1945 First child, Max Hastings, born.

1945–51 Becomes Editor of *Harper's Bazaar* magazine.

1951 Second child, Clare Hastings, born.

1952 *In the Mink*, her only novel, published.

1953–57 Writes for the *Sunday Express* – 'The Anne Scott-James Page'.

1957–59 Writes for the *Sunday Dispatch* – 'The Anne Scott-James Page'.

1959 Writes for the *Daily Express* – 'The Anne Scott-James Page'.

1960 Anne crosses the street and becomes a columnist on the *Daily Mail*, sharing an office with Bernard Levin.

1960 Asked to appear as 'expert witness' in the *Lady Chatterley* trial.

1961 Divorced from Macdonald Hastings.

1964 Succeeds journalist Nancy Spain on the BBC radio panel show *My Word*, with Frank Muir, Denis Norden and Dilys Powell.

1967 Marries Osbert Lancaster, cartoonist, and moves into Osbert's home in Eaton Square.

1968 Starts a series on gardening for *Queen* magazine, which launches her second career as a gardening writer.

1971 *Down to Earth*, first gardening book, published by Michael Joseph.

1974 *Sissinghurst: The Making of a Garden* published by Viking.

1977 *The Pleasure Garden: An Illustrated History of British Gardening*, with Illustrations by Osbert Lancaster, published by John Murray.

1978 Becomes a member of the Council of the Royal Horticultural Society and a judge for the Chelsea Flower Show.

Anne continues to write books on gardening into her nineties.

1981 *The Cottage Garden* published by Allen Lane.

1983 *Glyndebourne: The Gardens* (with Christopher Lloyd) published by Peterhouse Press.

1984 *The Language of the Garden* published by Viking.

1986 Osbert dies.

1988 *The Best Plants For Your Garden* published by Conran Octopus.

1989 *The British Museum Book of Flowers* (with Ray Desmond and Francis Wood) published by The British Museum.

1991 *Gardening Letters to my Daughter (with some replies by Clare Hastings)* published by Michael Joseph.

1993 *Sketches from a Life* published by Michael Joseph.

2005 Features on *Desert Island Discs.*

2009 Dies 13 May in Winchester, Hampshire.

The Anne Scott-James Page

My mother was a career journalist, at that glorious time when 'journalist' was not a dirty word. Fake news was unthinkable and the paparazzi had yet to be invented. To work on a 'daily' was romantic, a grand ambition, the papers to be relished and poured over, and journalists were welcomed and cheered rather than gazed at with suspicion and derision.

Anne would have been deeply depressed to hear there was such a thing as the Leveson inquiry. She herself was a very moral character, not in a puritanical way – she was produced as an 'expert witness' on behalf of the defence during the *Lady Chatterley* trial. But she was a passionate believer in the truth. She disliked any form of lying, and would rather have missed her stop than got off the bus without paying. Anne also believed that writers should take time to check their facts, and was utterly dismissive of anyone who didn't.

In 1953 she was hired by editor Harold Keeble to write an article for the *Sunday Express*. The article was about Queen Mary, who had recently died. It was popular. Anne was commissioned again, and then again. It was not long before she was employed to fill her own page. This was to appear every Sunday; she was to be their woman's editor, with the brief to inform and entertain the female reader. The *Sunday Express* boasted in 1954 a heady readership of nearly four million – a circulation today's papers could only dream of. Reaching this audience every week meant Anne had become a very serious player.

Called 'The Anne Scott-James Page', it set the bar for a new form of writing. I have often thought that with a couple of name changes, it would be simple to place Anne's column in a newspaper today and few readers would notice the differences. Topics that were on-trend in 1953 seem extremely familiar today.

She appealed to her readers to challenge her, thus involving them in the column and creating quite a feisty in-box, but, most important of all, she was allowed free rein. The weekly page was filled with her pithy opinions on children, food (rationing only really came to an end in 1954, nine years after the end of the war), interiors, fashion, beauty, travel and some political comments, all squashed in together. A piece on eyebrow tweezing made way for an interview with Françoise Sagan, which would then lead to an opinion on childbirth. All in all, it made for a rollicking read.

If she felt the subject deserved it, then the whole column could be written around a single issue, or she could fill the page with short quotes, musings and a photograph. Cross-pollination across topics seems rare now. A fashion editor is unlikely to air views on the NHS alongside a piece on the season's belts (a freedom they would doubtless relish).

As woman's editor, her brief was to appeal to female readers, and her writing assumed that her reader was informed and intelligent. The pieces never slipped into the banal, and fashion dictates of the season were dealt with in a brisk, informative style. Anne's writing was anything but ponderous. She was a great believer in engaging her reader.

The columns were certainly driven by her views, but she was aware that they should not be used to promote personal problems or stoke vanity. The reader – not the ego of the writer – was central. I think it is this that makes them so entertaining. It clearly created a connection. It didn't matter to Anne if readers agreed with her views or not – the more controversy the better, and the columns had to be topical. She was an acute observer, with a no-nonsense streak, and could cut to the chase in a couple of sentences. She also possessed a strong sense of irony (which could be used to punishing effect in the home, but worked like a charm in print).

All her work was produced on small Olivetti typewriters. Which were changed every now and again when a newer model came in. The first were black and upright, to be replaced with a later portable version in a rather pretty blue. Electric was never a consideration. Anne did not bother with touch-typing, but the two fingers she did use went tap-tapping away at an impressive rate. I really miss that wonderful staccato sound that comes from an old-fashioned typewriter, and the merry 'ting' at the end of a line. Changing the ribbon was also part of the charm: you could turn those ribbons over and round, reusing them several times, getting black, inky fingers in the process.

When my mother was very aged, finding new ribbons became quite the saga, the shops having moved on to stock computers and keyboards, mediums she never, to her chagrin, got to grips with. (I also remember the joy of Tipp-Ex, a thick white substance used to paint over typing errors, Anne using the very unsatisfactory brush to daub over any mistakes; but the liquid only remained smooth for a couple of applications – after a few days it would dry out, becoming unusable.)

Anne's handwriting was dire, and not improved by speed-writing during interviews. She never learned shorthand, and was wedded to a small notebook, always the same size and type, filled with thoughts and jottings. They were dated, with her address, on the front page of each one, and filled with a variety of topics. It could be a shopping list – melon, tonic, zip for Clare, blue dye and (at the end of this particular list – intriguing) 15 pints cream; a list of Ideas for stories – 'Shock treatment for infidelity', 'Is the corner shop cashing in?', 'How satisfying is France?', 'Smoking v. peanuts'; or a list of interviewees.

I particularly enjoy this one, composed before a trip to Paris: 'Bardot, Jean Seberg, Belmondo?' Sometimes a page was simply 'to do': 'Shoes ordered Nov. 22, fix net curtains, start column.'

The notebook and biro were part of her DNA, never far from the centre of operations, which consisted of a small desk (kept in a state of pristine order), and her handbag, which might as well have been permanently attached to her arm. 'Where's my bag?', was her cry of panic. It was probably a yard away. It certainly would never have strayed as far as the next room.

When she died, I had her bag cremated alongside her, as it seemed that in death, when crossing the Styx, she would have been lost without it. I kept a lipstick (she went in for rather vibrant pinks); it rolls around in a drawer, recalling her face to me more vividly than a photograph, where she was always rather posed, the photos usually set-ups for some publication or another.

Strong on common sense, and short on whingeing. She was brought up to be self-reliant. There was no time for self-pity. Life is messy, hers often was, but problems were dealt with pragmatically. Her mantra, often repeated to me, 'We weren't put on this earth to have fun' sounds rather brutal when you read it, but it resonated to me in a very positive way. If you don't expect fun, you are inclined to enjoy it all the more when it comes your way. This cheery phrase was usually uttered with a short, slightly humorless laugh, but it made me think, and making you think was important. As important in the home as on the page.

Introducing Anne Scott-James

13 December 1953

THE WOMAN'S ANGLE – IS IT A FLEET STREET MYTH?

You hear an awful lot of talk about the Woman's Angle. In newspapers and magazines – and in advertising, radio and politics – the powers that be are always competing to build up the 'woman's interest'. But are we really such peculiar birds? Can't we – who, in having babies, go through the rawest human experience next to a bayonet charge – stand up to an honest undoctored fact or two?

And are our tiny minds so pin-pointed on the boudoir and the sink that we want corners in the press and on the radio all to ourselves, where news, politics, travel, books, and so on, are strained through a filter to make them sweeter and more palatable?

The old division of HE going out to work and SHE (practically illiterate) waiting on him and then washing-up and knitting is (if it ever existed) dying out more than fast.

You don't have to be a feminist (I'm not) to know that, in the UK alone, 7 million women are in work and millions of men for whom there are no statistics help with children and the house.

THE TEST

Only the old-fashioned politician still believes that kissing a baby will win him a vote. Only an old-fashioned columnist believes that a cooing voice wins women readers.

What will I be doing with this page, with a column of my own? Am I hoping to interpret life, love, events through a woman's eyes? Not on your life. My aim is much more limited.

There are certain bits of life which *are* strictly and legitimately feminine, certain practical interests as special to women as football and all things mechanical to men. First of all I would put:

FASHION I like to report fashion in the same newsy, critical way as a sports reporter writes on football. I shall not pretend that all the fashion I see is marvellous. Nor shall I tell you how to dress to get a husband – that's your job. Mine is to see and sift fashion all over the world and give you the pickings.

BEAUTY As above. I hate ultra-sexy beauty tips, cranky diets and regimes that take all day. But new products, make-ups and hair-do's are just my meat.

SHOPPING Most women love shopping, most men detest it. When I was a child, if something had gone wrong at home, my mother used to say, 'Never mind, let's go shopping,' and I've inherited her belief that shopping is a solace.

CHILDREN My only theory about children is that the less theories you have about them the better. I am violently against rigid regimes, a lot of psychology, mothers who won't let their children get away from them, parents who sacrifice themselves completely for their young.

FOOD Surprise, surprise! I think English cooking is the best in the world. No, not the filthy stuff you get in cafés, hotels and many restaurants. But English private house and farmhouse cooking.

THE HOME This time – complaint, complaint! Englishwomen are the most stick-in-the-mud decorators in the world. I am not one of those who love all things American, but I find the American's attitude to her home stimulating and fresh. She likes to change the furniture, to try new curtains, to repaint and reupholster. In this matter I'm English, and lazy, but plan to improve.

I'll be reporting week by week on what's new and what's on the horizon, discussing other women's problems and other women's lives and speaking about the injustices that rankle.

Small Anne, summer 1918.

Anne and Health

Ill health was to define Anne's personality. It dogged her from her childhood through to old age. Not her own. She was one of the fittest women I have ever known. As she became older bits gave way, but she coped with her own aches and pains without complaint. If she was ever ill, I wouldn't hear anything about it until the crisis had passed. This stoicism covered everything from a bad cold to a broken hip.

Her own mother, Violet, had not been strong, often taking to her bed. She suffered from phobias and fears. These included a terror of thunderstorms, which, apparently, would cause her to tremble and dash round the house like a madwoman. Violet too had a literary bent, contributing a 'London Letter' to the *Yorkshire Post*. I have the usual sepia photograph showing a very pretty young woman, but I never knew her, as she died ten years before I was born.

Anne's sister had died at the age of fifty, so again I never came into contact with her. Another Alice in Wonderland beauty, only known from a couple of snapshots. The Scott-James family were not keen on preserving their image.

As soon as she was old enough Anne spent every hour looking after her brother, John, who was two years younger. Violet wasn't up to it. He had been born suffering from *petit mal*. This meant that many times a day he would suffer an epileptic fit and lose consciousness for a few seconds. In those few seconds, he might break a cup, fall over a piece of furniture or collide into a wall. While he was outside Anne's was the arm that held him up, preventing his falls. Doctors had decreed that there was nothing that could be done for him. John became her primary concern. Holidays with friends ,sporting activities – any ideas of independent fun – were abandoned. She loved him 'with an almost maternal love'.

During his teenage years his illness developed into *grand mal*, which sounds worse, but meant he could be more independent, as a serious attack might come after a considerable interlude. Mother said he was without fear, and would insist on riding his bike and going to the cinema alone. Once, in the war, when Violet moved from London to the country, John stole off for two days and joined the army. He was brought back home by a young lieutenant, saying 'I'm afraid there has been a mistake.' Poor John was crushed by the disappointment. For some time he came to help Anne with her cottage garden, as he was not up to any sort of regular work.

Apparently this was one of the few times that my father came into his own. Mother saying he was 'good with odd people'.

John died at forty, not from epilepsy but from lung cancer, and Anne was bereft. She was keen to point out that loving John was not a one-way street, he empathized with her problems, and was the person she would turn to in troubled times. There is no doubt that John's illness had a huge influence on Anne. The suppressed nervous side of her personality, I am sure, must have whestarted with the worry of watching John, and the stress of remaining alert in case of a seizure.

She remained throughout her life very tolerant of illness in others. When my stepfather, Osbert, was ill, she was tireless in her support – and he was not easy to be with. A stroke left him cross and frustrated, but she never complained about this change from his normal, exuberant personality. She loved him in sickness and in health. After his stroke Osbert too would sporadically lose consciousness. The flat was crowded with furniture and china and Anne must have felt that life had come full circle. Only this time she hadn't the physical strength to hold anyone up. Anne was used to recognizing the signs prior to a collapse, and was usually quick enough to break his fall, so they would land in a heap on the floor together. This was not without amusement. Once they were giving a small dinner for friends in the cottage. O got up, only to descend on to the floor, blocking the only door to the rest of the house. Rather than attempt to move him – 'He'll be fine, no, really, just leave him' – Mother simply provided a velvet cushion for his head, and nipped round the outside of the house when she needed to access the kitchen. Osbert recovered sufficiently to carry on chatting, while lying prone on the floor, and it was generally felt that the incident had added charm to the evening.

In later years, as Osbert became more incapacitated, Anne had to learn to cope with his nurses. Life in the home-hospital had begun. For someone who needed solitude this was a nightmare. There were day and night nurses, provided on rota by an agency. She grew to rely on and indeed to like a lot of them, but the general chatter wore her out. Catering for them all drained her too and she was constantly marvelling at their biscuit consumption. 'What do you think, dear? If I bought a hundredweight would they go soft? I tried to keep a pack in the back of the cupboard for Osbert's tea, but the packet disappeared. I might keep one in my underwear drawer. Do you think they will respect that?' Biscuits seemed to rule her life: she would apparently often nip off to the corner shop after supper to locate a packet – 'in the same way some people take an evening walk with the dog'.

Osbert's illness meant that he hated to be alone for a second. He wanted to know where she was all the time. Another room was too far away. He was depressed and demanding, although Anne tried in every way possible to cheer him along. It was exhausting and, for both of them, just terribly sad. When he died she missed him unspeakably. Work remained her salvation. Anne was commissioned to write a gardening book, *The Best Plants For Your Garden*, and it kept her sane for the initial year after his death.

Several years after Osbert died, Mother found a new companion to share holidays and suppers with. His name was Paul Willert, and he had been a prominent figure in the French oil and gas industries. During the war he was a Group Captain in the RAF and undertook missions for military intelligence which involved contact with the French Resistance. He was awarded the Croix de Guerre with palm, and also appointed to the Légion d'honneur. Paul was another stalwart of the Garrick, where, according to the broadcaster Sir Robin Day, he was commonly known as 'The Spy'. I have a delicious typed note from Mother, sent to me before a dinner at the Garrick, hosted by Paul. It lists the guests, with a one-liner for each one. It was headed 'Guests for Paul's dinner – most of them rather shady', and reads like a gathering for an Agatha Christie novel. 'Very shady White Russian Prince . . . Old flame of Paul's, tell Nick to beware . . . she's his 4th wife, clever doctor . . . he's terribly right wing, knew Osbert's set . . . a business partner of the poor, naive Stewart . . .' And, at the end of the list, 'French. Very pretty, will dress in something unbelievably outré, possibly half naked, so don't lag behind.' Mother was always keen on letting me know who was who – sort of. I am still recovering from a pre-dinner introduction to the late historian John Cornforth, 'John Cornforth, eighteenth-century architecture – my daughter, Clare,' and she swanned off leaving a silent vacuum as I dredged my mind for a suitable response.

Paul was recently widowed and lived within striking distance of her flat near the King's Road. For a few years they kept each other company. Mother was thrilled to have found someone who needed cutlets and conversation, and they would disappear on holidays to his house up in the Pyrenees near Pau, or sometimes abroad for a city break. Paul was utterly charming, cultured and devoted to Anne, but he was also getting on in years. His house was a hazard. The vertical line of stairs from the kitchen to the sitting room was lethal, and to see them tottering off together always made me worry for their safety. It did not take long before Mother was back on the care roster. Paul became forgetful and started to need more day-to-day help. Of course this was a natural turn of events, as he was in his eighties when they met, but it still struck me as unfair.

Anne accepted life's blows with extraordinary fortitude, and she did have many years coping as a carer. This goes a long way towards explaining why her mantra was always – 'We weren't put on this earth to have fun.'

25 April 1954

HOW'S YOUR HYPOCHONDRIA?

DO YOU take sleeping pills ?

DO YOU have little fetishes about vitamins? . . . calcium? . . . daily walks? . . . cold baths? . . . tonics? . . .

DO YOU try out digestive remedies, while ignoring your doctor's advice about what and much to eat?

DO YOU ever take your temperature to find out it's only normal?

DO YOU count calories ? . . . weigh yourself every day?

ARE YOU knowledgeable about new drugs and treatments from other countries?

DO YOU fuss if you get to bed very late, or have less than eight hours sleep?

I present my Seven Symptoms of Hypochondria. It comes to light because my personal spring-cleaning effort has been to chuck out the old bottles in the bathroom.

Though we are an indecently healthy family – which buys less than average from the chemist – I found that our bathroom medicine chest contained no fewer than forty-two pots, tubes, boxes, and bottles (most of them remnants of ancient prescriptions whose purpose was lost long ago).

'If there are forty-two bottles in our small cupboard,' I thought, 'what a load most of our friends must carry.' Because most of the people I know are becoming as health-crazy as the Americans.

Words like metabolism, neurosis, calorie, barbiturate are part of their everyday chit-chat. Pills, diets and doctors' addresses are swapped round like recipes.

And any book about a doctor is a sure-fire bestseller before it gets off the press.

When a hearty, healthy, globe-trotting friend of mine told me last week he was taking a course of 'Remedial Relaxation Exercises', it brought home to me that the new disease of fearing disease is getting out of hand.

5 August 1956

EQUALITY FROM DOCTORS

Those who would like to nationalize all medicine on the grounds that there is one health law for the rich and one for the poor can stop worrying.

There is a growing tendency among doctors to treat private patients with the same offhand grandeur they used to reserve for the National Health.

I am one of thousands of professional people who pay for medical attention, *not* for snobbish reasons, *not* because I think NHS treatment is inferior (I know it is often first class) but for reasons of time.

If you have the eyes, teeth, digestions and so on of yourself and a few children to keep in order, and you also do a job, it is just not possible to queue for medical attention on what may mount up to several days a month.

But doctors have now become so indifferent to anybody's workload but their own – in short, so frightfully conceited – that there will soon be no point in paying for an appointment. And, frankly, I shall be glad to save the money. It is now commonplace for a specialist to keep you waiting three-quarters of an hour after your time.

'Doctor will see you now,' says his secretary at last, with condescension, as if you had come to sell him some samples. Not a word of apology, and you pay five guineas.

GPs, who used to come to your home, now offer you an inconvenient appointment several days ahead for a semi-urgent trouble.

Of course, doctors always have the last laugh, because while you have been waiting they *may* have been saving valuable life. If you grumble, they give you a look which says, 'Do you really want me to bind up your finger while the life of some tiny boy is at stake?'

Well, I don't believe that if all our lives were permanently at stake it would account for half those hours in waiting rooms. Come off it, doctors, you are human, not divine. And we work hard, too.

Glam in furs,
by Cecil Beaton for *Vogue*.

Anne and Beauty

Anne did not spend hours at the mirror. But she would no more think of leaving the house without her make-up complete than of walking down Fleet Street naked. She was always immaculately made up. In the early years Elizabeth Arden was her foundation of choice, and mascara came from a small box containing a hard block of black stuff, requiring a bit of spit and a hearty rub with a little brush – flat, not spiral. Alongside this was a small pink pot that contained a cream turquoise-green eyeshadow. This was a colour she favoured all her life. A black pencil was used as eyeliner (slight flick at the corner), and to add shape to the eyebrows. Her powder too was quite utilitarian, administered with a round, rather hard puff, instead of a swansdown wrapped in a chiffon hanky, a fabulous accessory favoured by my aunt.

Anne spent little or no money on a beauty regime. Pond's cold cream was her go-to pot for everything of a basic nature, including cleansing and moisturizing, and she would visit either Arden or Harrods for the once-a-year facial.

She loved lunching in the sun, under a large umbrella, but even on holiday I never saw her lying out in it. She was not interested in being 'tanned', and her face was usually shaded with a straw something. The shade, Pond's and a flannel and water were all she needed to maintain a flawless complexion.

There was also the weekly visit to the hairdresser's for a shampoo and set. I am not sure who attended to her hair in the 1950s – Harrods, probably. Aldo's in South Kensington took over in the 1960s, when I would accompany Mother for a shampoo and the new, revolutionary, blow-dry. In later life Peter Jones filled the gap. Anne favoured a perm, and had perfected the art of home hairdressing in between salon visits. Rollers, be they bristle, heated or foam, were wound with the aplomb of a professional, and kept in place with a tasteful chiffon scarf (red). The brush and comb set was by Mason Pearson. During the early sixties Mother owned a 'piece' – a tremendously chic bob of hair on a thin Alice band, probably provided by Aldo. It came out in the evenings, and meant you could create an on-trend hair-do without the faff of going back in the late afternoon for a 'comb out'. The 'piece' remained a firm favourite for some time, until eventually it was retired and Mother reverted to the status quo.

It was during her time on the *Sunday Express* that Christmas tended to come early, with 'gifts' sent from the various make-up houses. These usually consisted of large satin-lined boxes tied with elaborate bows and filled with a huge selection of the latest products. I particularly recall a big basketwork swan, the hollow in its back overflowing with bath cubes and powders. Encased in cellophane, it was the most marvellous thing I had ever seen – and is probably the reason I am drawn to baskets of any shape or form to this day. The boxes never seemed to end up being used, nor did the contents make their way to any bathroom cupboard. I was kept well away from them, so I suspect they were re-gifted to secretaries at the paper. (Why were they sent to the flat and not the office? I have no idea.)

When she reached her mid-fifties I would sometimes catch her in the mirror pulling up the sides of her cheeks, in that way known to all women (and men) of a 'certain age'. Catching the elusive glimpse of youth – 'I'd just like to get rid of that bit, dear.'

She was interested in plastic surgery, and wrote articles about the newest techniques for the paper, which had clearly concentrated her mind on the idea. She would never have done it. It smacked too much of self-indulgence. Anne would have felt guilty spending that much money on herself. Some women really don't need it anyway, and she was one. Her eyes, which were grey, kept their sparkle and her skin never really gave way. Even into her nineties you would know, just by a glance, that here was a woman who had been a beauty in her youth, and she knew it too. Secure in her looks, she would still remind me of this fact from time to time, in case I had failed to notice. Her friends often mentioned it to me as well – Vivien Leigh's name was brought up as a reference point – brains and beauty, a lethal combo. Anne also knew deportment was important, and in old age would hold herself arrow-straight as she walked, even as her steps became slower and smaller.

Diet pieces appeared regularly on her page, and Anne left her readers in no doubt that the solution was to eat less. I was regularly challenged if I started to look a bit tubby, and in her declining years she also kept an eagle eye on my daughter, questioning me closely if she felt a stray pound or two had appeared. As we are both by design on the thin side, we weathered the remarks. The following turned up – written, interestingly, in the back of a recipe scrapbook Anne was in the process of compiling. The search for the perfect onion tart had led her mind to cogitate on measures of a different kind. It was headed 'Advancing Years'.

The greatest enemy is weight. Affecting one's happiness, walk, elegance. I am revolted by rolls of fat around the middle. The skin gets blemished – freckles on the hands I like, but an odd freckle on the face can look like a dirty mark. A wart or a mole is horrid. Greying hair one is no longer aware of. Greying eyebrows (which often go first) can be retouched every morning. How lucky to grow old in an age of so much make-up and unashamed artificiality. Knees get inflexible. Osteoarthritic bumps on knuckles. Very shocked to get one on my writing finger at fifty-six. Everyone says how beautiful you were ten years ago.

Anne kept a small bottle of Floris bath oil on the side of the bath, and always used Yardley's Lavender soap and occasionally a bath cube. The lurid green of Wiberg Pine Essence also had a place, but not, I think, until the 1960s.

Her scent of choice was Joy, created by Jean Patou in 1929. It takes just a whiff to remind me of Mother leaving for an evening, engulfed in that glamorous, heady waft of roses and jasmine.

I have mentioned all these cosmetic items by name, not because they were a rarity at the time, but because I think they are informative. Essentially she never changed her look, or her products. Once she had found a formula that suited her she stuck with it, which is why I can remember them all so well. She marshalled her dressing table and bathroom with that same need for order which ran through her life. The only hint I ever got of the nervousness beneath all this control was that she bit her nails, a habit that stayed with her throughout her time at the *Express* and the *Mail*. Not in the truly disgusting way that some people adopt, but she kept nibbling away, until eventually she managed to break the habit by applying false ones. Anne also smoked – but then, didn't everyone? Rothmans or Benson & Hedges, since you ask.

8 May 1955

YOU TOO CAN BE BEAUTIFUL WITH THESE GIMMICKS

You'd think by the number of letters I get about beauty, grooming and the art of being magnetically attractive, that no one had touched the subject before.

Yet millions of words have been written about it.

Don't mistake me and think that the search for glamour bores me. On the contrary, I am a monomaniac about my appearance – spend *hours* at the mirror trying new cheekbones or a different parabola for my eyebrows.

It's just I don't think there is much new to be said about it. If you don't know how to exploit your personality, you can't be trying.

However, 'in response to many requests', as the band leaders say, I've done a simple summing-up of what I really believe about beauty. Some of it's old, some of it's new, but all of it works. I hereby present some Tested Rules for being a *femme fatale*.

The *femme fatale* must . . .

SPEND A FORTUNE ON HER HAIR

Spend more than you can afford on having your hair done often and well. Save on something that matters less, like the children's education.

In the news Every kind of colouring, from bleaches to dyes to rinses that last just a few hours.

HAVE MAGNETIC EYES

Beautiful eyes eclipse every other feature. With them you

can get away with having quite a slabby face. Pile on the mascara, darken your eyebrows and outline your eyes with pencil. Use twice as much as you've ever dared.

Idea that works Eyedrops before a party – they give an almost alcoholic glitter.

HAVE A SOFT SKIN

Dry skin is more ageing than any other factor; and is strangely prevalent in this moist island. Some modern make-ups are drying: avoid them. The sun is drying: use a little oil as protection. Hard water is drying: use a cream after washing your face.

Warning Take care of the delicate skin under your eyes. Once it sags, you've had it.

BE REASONABLY SLENDER

Stress 'reasonably' because you need not have the skeleton measures of a model. Many men do not care for jutting bones. But you mustn't be fat, or walk with a waddle.

Hard fact A fat girl must eat less, there's no other way.

GIVE OFF SPARKS

Sickly, languorous creatures may have swept the board in other ages, but not in the 1950s. The Ava Gardeners, the Lollobrigidas are electrically alive.

Best source of vitality Sleep: a long night, a Sunday in bed, or frequent cat-naps.

NOT BE OVER-CONSCIOUS

You clean your teeth – but don't think about them all day. Same way, make up your face with love and care and then forget it. Practise every art of make-up, clothes and grooming and then get on with something else.

If at the end of it you're still not a *femme fatale*, I would count your losses and go for something different.

17 February 1956

WOULD YOU LIKE TO BUY YOURSELF A NEW FACE?

One branch of science is expanding furiously, and it has no sinister undertones. Cosmetic surgery. It is now reputable and unsecretive. Every year, more and more women (and men) have noses straightened, defects corrected, faces made younger, to the benefit of their happiness and health.

I have just read a book on *Cosmetic Surgery* by one of the crack surgeons in Paris, Dr Jean Bolvin.

As the book impressed me greatly, and as the French surgeons are supposed to be the best in the world at the job (the French *care* most about beauty), I came to Paris to see him. Dr Bolvin has fixed the faces of celebrities from every country on earth. He started life as a painter and sculptor, so he views each face with an artist's as well as a doctor's eye.

SUCCESSFUL?

'Which operations are the most successful? I asked.

'All are successful,' he said. 'We know enough about it now that we have no failures. The chief operations are for the nose, eyes, facial lines, ears, neck, but much the most common operation is to the nose. I have done noses for people of all ages, including my own daughter, who is nineteen. Her nose was rather broad.'

'At what age should a woman who wants to stay young-looking have cosmetic surgery?'

'It is best to have it young, say at forty or less. I cannot get perfect results if the lines are set too deep. The first operation is usually for the lines under the eyes. These are the first to appear, and if they are removed a woman looks, five, ten or even fifteen years younger.

'Do the operations need to be repeated?'

'The eye operation no. Other operations have to be repeated, say, five years afterwards.'

RISK?

'Is there a risk that a woman will have an altered expression? We all know the look of a bad facelift.'

'Not by my methods. Some surgeons merely drag the skin tighter. I take away the fat underneath'.

WHAT ABOUT THE PRICE?

It costs up to £300. I have had many patients in very humble jobs and I charge according to their means.

Well there are the facts. They are encouraging and I believe them to be true.

Yet, looking gloomily at my own face in the glass when I got home, I decided to stick for a while to the status quo.

27 May 1956

AGONY, BUT WORTH IT

This is going to be one of my days for telling the truth. You *can't* lose weight or improve your figure *without hardship*. No, it takes toil and effort to lose weight, and perhaps only women have the willpower for it. But make the effort, and you can lose it quickly.

THE FIRST WAY

And the more important, is by diet. This is the only way to lose an appreciable amount of weight, to lose it quickly and to lose it all over.

THE SECOND WAY

Which will work down local fat spots and also tone the muscles, is by specialist exercise.

Now, any low-calorie diet will get your weight down. Many good ones have been published and there are no sensational new principles. But, as you may not have found a diet to your liking, I have had a two-week spring-cleaning diet worked out for you which should improve your skin, your hair and your health, along with your figure.

One day liquids only, to cleanse and spring-clean your whole system

Two days on a 1,000-calorie diet

Four days on a 1,250-calorie diet of dairy foods, fruit, vegetables and fish

One week still on 1,250 calories but including meat

It only remains for me to suggest thst while you diet and exercise to improve your summer figure you should drag your husband along with you.

After all, nobody on a diet can watch another person shovelling in those buttery new potatoes, powdered with chopped mint, without wishing the dish was poisoned. And, after all, he can look pretty awful on the beach too. Yes, face it together, ache for ache, tomato for tomato, beaten-up egg with beaten-up egg.

Two weeks agony . . . but worth it.

Modelling a dress from 1907 for a book by fashion
historian Doris Langley Moore.

Anne and Fashion

Mother was tall, just shy of six foot, unfashionably well educated (St Paul's Girls' School, followed by a scholarship to Somerville College, Oxford) and considered a 'beauty'. So if you had to guess which skill gave Anne her entrée into journalism, I do not suppose that knitting would be high on the list. But we all start somewhere. Swearing that she was only happy when purling, she applied and was taken on at *Vogue* as assistant to the knitting pattern editor. On the way home from the interview she purchased *First Steps to Stylish Knitting* and, with three days to go before starting work, set about learning how to knit stylishly.

It was not considered enough simply to answer enquiries or check a pattern. Readers sent in their duff woollies, complete with holes and missed stitches. Anne would then take home the sad bundles of wool offerings, unpick and reknit, before they were parcelled up and returned. (Hard to imagine Anna Wintour, even in her early days, surrounded by balls of wool in contrasting shades.) Mother retained the skill throughout her life, and could knock out the most complicated patterns without pause. Indeed, she kept up the knitting until her marriage to Osbert Lancaster, who found the image of her sitting opposite him needles in hand depressing.

In April 1945, fresh from her position as woman's editor on *Picture Post*, Anne was offered the job of editor for the glossy fashion magazine *Harper's Bazaar*. This proved an unsatisfying period in her career. Fashion was still suffering from shortages resulting from the war. Rationing was still in place, and the designers and creative talents had hardly had time to re-establish themselves. But it was not just the practicalities that proved such a problem for her.

Although she loved clothes, and enjoyed discovering new talent for the magazine (Elizabeth David was first published on her pages), she found the actual world of fashion stifling and became desperate to break out. She needed more of an outlet for her opinions and intellect, and thought she should and could do better.

In the early 1970s, as I started my first job in the fashion department of *Harpers & Queen* magazine, Mother warned me against staying too long. (At this point I had barely been at my desk a week, and indeed was literally still trying to locate Bond Street.)

Anne wrote this to herself in 1986:

I hate myself when I am not well groomed. This raises the hoary question, for whom do women dress – for men, for other women or for themselves? In my case, it is largely for self-respect.

Of course, when I was younger I dressed partly to attract men, partly to make a splash in society, but always also for myself. I have never spent much time on myself, preferring ready-made to made-to-measure clothes (which involve tedious fittings), and always choosing a quick and punctual hairdresser. But the feeling of well-being when I am well dressed is deeply, not superficially, important to me. There is an aesthetic reward to it. When the colours are right and the fit and proportions good I can think better and work better and am altogether more agreeable.

Although fashions come and go, Anne did, as we all do, have her uniform. In the early days, suits played an essential part, a well-cut wool jacket and matching skirt, often worn with a pussycat-bow blouse. She was not afraid of colour – a plain navy suit might well be set off by a shocking pink blouse, and she loved a red coat. Although she did occasionally wear trousers, this was rare. Through the decades she most often wore skirts (favouring pleats and plaid) and shirts. I don't think she ever owned a dress. There was a kaftan moment (everyone had a kaftan moment), obviously only worn for the evening, bought from a shop called Savita in Knightsbridge. They were embroidered and embellished with little mirrors and I loved them but, they were not her best fashion moment. Too much unstructured fabric. Anne looked much more glamorous in long evening skirts, and she was glamorous. Caring as much about her appearance at ninety as she did in her youth.

Wide belts were a constant, as was a belted wool coat. The shoulder lines might be set in or dropped, the length could vary (always on or just below the knee for the day), but she knew that with her height and long legs, it was flattering and chic to break at the waist.

Mother did not hoard jewellery, but there was always a brooch on her lapel, or maybe a bunch of artificial flowers pinned at the neck. Large fake pearls were a feature, and clip-on earrings, again large pearls or gold discs. Anne never had her ears pierced, although she sometimes asked me whether I thought it a good idea. (As I had three holes in my ears I obviously did, but she was nervous about making the decision.)

She often bemoaned the fact that the men in her life were not great jewellery-givers. My father certainly wouldn't have thought of it, and Osbert was absolutely hopeless at remembering birthdays, or even buying for Christmas. Indeed, he even forgot to bring a wedding ring to their marriage ceremony at Chelsea registry office, bizarrely thinking it wouldn't be needed. There was a great kerfuffle as Myfanwy Piper (John Piper's wife) and Anne struggled frantically to prise any ring they could from their fingers, so the ceremony might continue. Competitive in everything, Mother noted: 'I got mine off first.' This is not to say Osbert was mean, it just didn't seem important. Every now and then, for no reason, he would come home flourishing a box from Mappin & Webb, making the gift all the more exciting for being unexpected; but it has to be said the occasions were rare.

Because of her height, Anne never wore heels – but she was proud of her long legs, thin ankles and very slim feet. She also had 'Greek toes'. The Italian shoe designer Ferragamo was apparently, the only person in Europe who understood a slim fit, and she rarely deviated, unless she was on a visit to the States – American shoe companies were also up to the mark when it came to the long, narrow shoe. Anne was no Imelda Marcos. I think the most pairs she would ever have at one time was about five (including one evening). Neatly lined up and fitted with shoe trees. I never saw her wear boots, except the short furry type if the weather was extreme. I certainly can't recall ever seeing her in gumboots, which is odd, as of course she was an avid gardener, but her outdoor shoes just became more robust. Again, I am not sure if she ever actually performed 'double digging', being more of the trowel and pruner persuasion. Still it shows an attention to appearance not even to own any. In old age, Mother did take to wearing plimsolls. 'Well, it's all right for you, dear. You are always style over comfort.'

Despite her long career looking at fashion, she did not have a bulging wardrobe. Maybe the war had taught her to be careful. When she bought a new shirt an old one went out, or was relegated to the cottage – she was not sentimental about hanging on to clothes, there was always a decent space between the hangers. Anne retained her interest and love of clothes throughout her life, and she really enjoyed shopping. In her dotage I would be summoned to accompany her around the King's Road, so she could keep on updating her wardrobe. Apparently her mother had instilled the concept that shopping was the answer to all life's ills, and she in turn instilled it in me.

She was dismayed when the department stores were taken over by franchises. Bemoaning the fact that Peter Jones no longer seemed to have a 'shirt' department, and that everything was chucked in together, Anne always said the stores had made life more complicated for the shopper, and she didn't want to walk around every floor to locate one specific item.

Anne did not have a coterie of friends from her fashion life, but three remained constant. Lionel Green, the founder of Windsmoor, the Italian couturier Emilio Pucci, and photographer Bert Hardy. This is not to say that she saw them with any great regularity once she left Fleet Street, but they were, like all true friends, able to reconnect immediately, even after an absence of years.

In the Fleet Street years Lionel was one of Mother's regular lunch dates. Windsmoor was located in Mayfair, and when Mother joined the *Sunday Express* was hitting the heights of success. Lionel gave her a much-prized wood and brass measuring stick, which had been attached to one of the cutting tables. A memento which she always treasured.

Bert Hardy, born in the East End, had worked with Mother on *Picture Post*, and she adored him. His wit and talent earned him a very special spot in her affections. She said that when they worked on assignments he always made the trips 'more of an adventure than a slog'. They must have seemed an unlikely pair, but, according to Anne, he had the charm to move mountains.

Emilio also seems to have had more charm than was good for her. I can truly say that the only time I ever saw her blush was when Emilio telephoned. Apparently there was nothing Emilio couldn't do. He spoke five languages, skied 'like a dream', had been an airline pilot, designed prints to die for, and that was all before calculating his title, the palazzo in Florence, or his Italian good looks into the equation. I think you could say Mother had a 'crush'. The last time they met was in 1986, after Osbert died, when Emilio came to London on a flying visit, and they spent an afternoon together, with Emilio apparently 'talking his head off, until 7 o'clock'. Mother had a marvellous collection of silk Pucci shirts. What ever happened to them I wonder? Probably donated to the Chelsea Oxfam shop, when I took my eye off the ball for a weekend.

This portrait was a wedding gift from
Felix Mann on Anne's marriage to my father.

IT DOESN'T MAKE SENSE

That when all the shops are having a difficult fashion season (the warm weather has stopped people buying), salesmanship in too many of them is worse than ever.

I went into one shop last week and asked if they had any polo-necked sweaters.

THE GIRL: We've only got yellow.

ME: As a matter of fact, it's yellow I want.

THE GIRL: Only size 34 left.

ME: That's my size.

THE GIRL: They're expensive – over £5.

ME (reckless): I don't mind the price.

THE GIRL: They're a very eggy yellow.

This beat me at last, and I went away. The so-called salesgirl had managed to UN-sell me the sweater I wanted to buy.

I suppose it saved her the trouble of packing up a parcel and writing a bill . . . and it meant she could get back to talking to the other salesgirls.

But it made me wonder what the shop was for.

I'LL CHAMPION THE FASHION FAKER

A string of seed pearls or a big fat choker of fake pearls? The big fat choker every time.

Because in fashion the words 'fake', 'imitation', 'copy' no longer carry a slur.

When I was a child it was a matter of morality to have everything real. If you couldn't afford a good fur coat or a genuine diamond brooch, you went without. Only cads wore artificial things.

But three great social changes have cracked this snobbery.

FIRST The levelling of incomes.

SECOND The onrush of science. Floods of plastics and synthetics, of new fabrics and finishes have poured out of the laboratories with brilliant new qualities which cry out to be used.

THIRD The pace of fashion has speeded up from a slow march to a sprint, so it is doubtful if you *want* your clothes to last for ever. Shoulders go out and in, skirts go up and down, accessories grow big and small, all with such rapidity that the 'good suit' which should last for years can become a liability.

So I give my blessing (rather to my own surprise) to Fakes in Fashion . . . whether they are diamonds the size of ducks' eggs, or really deceitful fakes, like manmade fabrics that are the spit image of real wool.

I give my blessing to the vast and wonderful range of synthetic fabrics, from the nylon that makes our stockings and lingerie to Orlon sweaters and pleated Terylene skirts. I like them for their essential modern qualities: the way they pack and pleat and resist those beastly moths.

I give my blessing to fake furs. A chunky fake fur sports jacket, a fake fur lining and collar to a topcoat, a fake fur leopard skirt, a fake fur Persian lamb stole – all yes, a hundred times yes.

12 December 1954

GIVE ME ONE WISH AND I'LL HAVE THE SHOPS FROM NEW YORK

Back from the handsome, charmless city, I flashed back over all the things I had seen. I asked myself what I'd import into Britain if I could choose One Thing.

I'd say: Bring me the shops.

It's not the goods I want; many of ours are as fine or better. It's the service the shops offer the customer.

I WANT to be able to go into a shop knowing I can buy a dress, skirt, slip that will fit me. Fashions are stocked in many sizes and several lengths, and once you know you take a tall 14 everything in that size fits you.

Even *dolls* are sized, so if you want to buy extra dolls' clothes, you can go into a shop and ask for a dolls' hat and coat set, size 1.

I WANT to be able to shop, sometimes, in the evenings. I think it is a disgrace that many of our West End shops should close at 5 o'clock, shutting their doors to women who work. There is no hour of the day or night when you can't buy things in New York. There is always a drugstore open selling everything from a cheeseburger to dental floss.

On Broadway, there's even a hairdresser that's open all night.

I WANT to have my presents deliciously boxed and packaged for no extra charge.

I WANT to read the shops' advertisements and know that the goods they show are really there.

I WANT to be served by salesgirls who know what they are selling and are fully acquainted with the qualities and prices of their stock.

But, oh, it was nice to get home to British politeness. I nearly kissed the Customs man.

But, oh, it was good to get home to British kindness. I'd like to adopt our greengrocer.

UNFAIR TO A FAVOURITE

Off my visiting list. Couturier Neil Roger. I went out to supper wearing my favourite dinner dress, which is black velvet with a fitted, nipped-in waist and a full bell skirt. I thought I looked divine. He appraised it with a professional eye. '*My dear,*' he said, '*the first sack dress I've seen.*'

A DARK CHALLENGER . . . COMES INTO YOUR LIFE

The colour of the season is the hardest colour in the world to wear. It's the colour that drains the life out of your face, that makes you look tired even when you feel terrific, that is dejected and dowdy, that puts ten years on your age.

The colour of the season is the kindest colour in the world. It's the colour that makes a plain woman elegant and a pretty woman superb. It's the colour that has the most mystery and sophistication, that brings out the best in other colours, that is the ideal setting for jewellery and delicious accessories.

I'M TALKING ABOUT BLACK
Tens of thousands of fashion-conscious women are going to wear black this winter, by day and by night.

Lovely . . . so long as they realize that black needs more know-how than any other fashion in the book.

IT NEEDS a new approach to make-up. Take the eye make-up you usually wear and double it. None of those subtle touches, please. And tons of mascara.

IT NEEDS an unorthodox hair-do. Last year's neat swept-back coiffure won't do at all – too severe. This year's wilder romantic coiffures *will* do . . . marvellously. For evening you might need the extra glow of a bit of fake colour in your hair; a chestnut or prune rinse if you're dark, a silver rinse for blondes.

IT NEEDS a lively hat. An all-black hat can cast deadening shadows. But a dotted veil will soften them. Or get away from black altogether – the prettiest hat I've seen in 1956 is made entirely of very small aquamarine feathers.

IT NEEDS a fabric with vitality. Black tweed rather than dull smooth wool, black velvet or lace rather than chiffon, which is always prettiest in pastel shades.

IT NEEDS brilliant accessories. Always earrings.

IT NEEDS assurance in the wearing. A quiet black suit is a certain bromide. A diffident little black dress is a sure, sure flop.

THE WORST-DRESSED WOMEN IN THE WORLD

Now that those of lists of Best-Dressed Women have fallen into disrepute, I am starting my own personal Fashion Award.

From time to time I shall publish a list of the Worst-Dressed Women in the World.

I think if will be much more useful than the other system. In the first place the Best-Dressed Women are usually chosen for snobbish reasons rather than true fashion. All sorts of ill-dressed Royal Persons get in to make the thing look classy.

Secondly, the women who really *are* well dressed, like the Duchess of Windsor, usually spend so much time and money on their clothes that their efforts are meaningless to you and me. (When all they really have to do is put themselves in the hands of Balenciaga and let him get on with the job.)

There's much more to be learnt from other people's mistakes – how not to choose a hat, how not to wear accessories.

Here, after a prolonged study of many hundreds of published photographs, is my Worst-Dressed List. Please note I haven't picked anyone who is badly dressed because of an unworldly temperament or a lack of money. I have tried not to hit below the belt. All these women lead sophisticated lives and could easily do better.

I select :

Mrs Eisenhower – for dressing like a little girl. The bangs and the bonnet, the 'ickle jacket and the full skirt, are more fit for the college girl on campus than the President's wife.

The Marchioness of Dufferin and Ava – for combining grapes, shamrock leaves, a cut collar, ankle straps and buttons on the fussiest outfit of the fifties. She wore it to the rehearsal of the Coronation.

Nancy Spain – for making every appearance an attack on fashion. Independent and likeable, she says she will wear what she jolly well pleases. But she is in the public eye and we all have to look at her – and, Nancy, *there are limits.*

Dr Edith Summerskill – for dressing like an old-style feminist, ignoring her chance to prove that women can be both feminine and able. Mannish hair, ugly accessories are an injustice to herself and us.

Greta Garbo – for being the most beautiful woman in the world and looking quite ugly. Dank hair, dark glasses, untidy scarf, armfuls of things to carry are no way to travel.

Mrs Walter Nell – for not knowing the classic rule. Look at yourself in the glass before you go out and see what you can take off. With earrings, necklace, and several competing clusters of flowers, there is just too much going on.

Janette Scott – for throwing away her gifts of prettiness and youth and overdressing. Mittens, dorothy bag, flowers, bo-peep dress, back interest, front interest, side interest may be eye-catching, but are not good fashion.

Anita Ekberg – for wearing a dress which is a bad fit (too tight all over) and ill-chosen for the occasion (*to meet the Queen*).

Lady Docker – for committing the cardinal sin of all-matching accessories. One hunk of leopard, good. Two hunks of leopard, plenty. Three hunks of leopard, overwhelming. And the coat is inches too long. Any local tailor would shorten it.

NOTES

Mamie Eisenhower (1896-1979) Wife of Dwight Eisenhower, President of the United States 1953-1961.

Maureen, Marchioness of Dufferin and Ava (1907-1998), A regular in the society pages, she became a director in the family business – the Guinness brewery – in 1949.

Nancy Spain (1917-1964) Broadcaster and journalist. Nancy died in a plane crash in 1964. My mother took over her role as one of the panellists on the radio show *My Word*.

Dr Edith Summerskill (1901-1980) Physician, ardent feminist, Labour politician and writer.

Greta Garbo (1905-1990) Film actress – and most beautiful woman in the world.

Mrs Walter Nell (1908-1987) Susan Bates, married to Walter, Chairman of the Express Dairy Co. (In 1958 they divorced and she married the actor Michael Wilding.)

Janette Scott Actress. Daughter of Thora Hird.

Anita Ekberg (1931-2015) Actress. Crowned 'Miss Sweden' in 1950. (Probably best known for her role as Sylvia in Federico Fellini's *La Dolce Vita*, 1960.)

Norah, Lady Docker (1906-1983) Married to Sir Bernard Docker. Fodder for gossip columns, they became known as 'The Dazzling Dockers'.

Anne outside her cottage in Berkshire.

Anne and Common Sense

Common sense and Anne went hand in hand. She would have made a very good magistrate. She was very intuitive about people, and was usually absolutely correct in her judgement.

Anne was quick to point out that brainpower and common sense were not the same thing: 'Very intelligent, dear, but no common sense.' The fact she had both contributed to her success.

1960 saw Penguin books summoned to the Old Bailey to answer the charge that it planned to publish an obscene article.

A book by D.H Lawrence called *Lady Chatterley's Lover*, written in 1928, was the subject. the four-letter words used by Lawrence a particular source of angst. Anne was called as one of a large group of erudite men and women as witnesses for the defence. It was noted in the book of the trial that she looked as if she had stepped out of the pages of *Vogue*.

COUNSEL FOR THE PROSECUTION: In your view has it any sociological or educational merits?

ANNE SCOTT-JAMES: Oh, yes, immense. I think it is extremely important in view of the time at which it was written. Lawrence was an iconoclast; he thought the times were stiff and stuffy, that sex was treated hypocritically, that money was the guard round love and human relationships, and he was smacking at it.

CP: From the point of view of sociological or education merits, what would be your view as to reading *Lady Chatterley's Lover* as Lawrence wrote it and the same book with all the parts relating to sex taken out of it?

AS-J: I would rather not see it published at all than published in an expurgated edition.

There then followed a terse exchange with the cross examiner, who attempted to belittle Anne's intellectual qualification to make a judgement on the book.

CP: Please don't think I am intending to be rude, but evidence as to the literary merit of this book is confined to experts – I only wondered, do you claim any particular qualifications to be a literary expert?'

AS-J: I think I do, yes.

CP: What? [Incredulously; and then] Of a *popular* kind ...

AS-J: What? Well, I was a classical scholar at Somerville College, Oxford.

CP: Not every classical scholar at Somerville College, Oxford, is a literary expert?

AS-J: No. It isn't a negligible qualification, though.

Actually, Anne was asked not as a literary expert, but as a writer on 'family problems and children'. The defence had considered that her common sense and insight into the mindset of her readers would prove valuable to the arguments. This fact was overlooked in the cross-examination – which did not daunt Anne a whit.

Common sense also meant taking charge of her changing circumstances. She sold her beloved cottage several years earlier than was really necessary. (I have no doubt that this is a perceived wisdom, and that *Saga* will have written many leaflets on the subject.)

After the sale, it was a regular occurrence to look out of our kitchen window around 9 a.m. on a Saturday to see a small red Ford turning into the driveway. My partner would put down his toast, utter the cry 'Plaid skirt alert!' and Mother would arrive at the door with a cheery 'just passing', which we always felt was stretching a point. Our own cottage backed on to my mother's and after functioning as a 'weekender' for sixty years, the pull of the M4 had become a habit just too strong to resist. All other activities would be put to one side, and we would go into full-on Anne mode.

Anne's opinion was always of interest, whether relating to personal fiascos, work dilemmas or political subjects. She could cut to the chase and process the available data very speedily and if she didn't know the answer she would say so, which is quite a rare talent. I often find myself saying 'What would Anne do?'

Common sense was vital for her first job, which was as agony aunt for a magazine called *Weldon's*. On arriving to work, she was issued with bundles of letters and sent home to write the replies. Letters on love lost and spots found, medical dilemmas and fashion problems were all considered and replies of length sent back. But as soon as Anne reached the bottom of the first batch, she returned them to *Weldon's* for posting, was paid and then subsequently resigned. Rather a pity, as I think her answers would have proved useful to their readers and this was an area where she would have been of considerable benefit.

You could always rely on mother's common sense in a domestic emergency. She would instinctively rise to the occasion, was unshockable, and was not afraid to take matters into her own hands. This was useful when it came to dealing with authority. She was fearless. On a holiday to Spain (I was theoretically in charge of the party) with Anne and my small daughter, there was a strike by baggage handlers. As we set foot on the tarmac it was clear the airport was in chaos. The queue was awesome. The heat and trauma got to me, and I passed out. In the time it took me to fall over, she had me propped in a corner, while she barged through the crowds, the Customs and passport control. Hitting the terminal, she then purchased a bottle of water and reversed her way back through the system to resuscitate and rescue me. As far as I know, no attempt was made to prevent her. (Well, good luck with that one. I would probably still be queuing.)

Similarly, she dismissed all protocol to extract my daughter (then about five) from hospital, a few days after an operation. I was working and couldn't get back in until the next morning to sign the paperwork. Anne just breezed along and removed her. 'Well, dear, she couldn't stay *there* any longer.' I am a martyr to authority. Anne the reverse.

In the last year of her life, I was visiting Mother, and the conversation turned to people you would like to meet up with again. Anne, rather surprisingly, said that the only person she would really like to talk to was her sister, Marie. My aunt had died before I ever knew or indeed met her.

Mother had never once mentioned her, or discussed her, except to say they weren't close, which funnily enough I had gathered. Apparently Marie had once asked her opinion about divorce, as she was considering it. Anne had come out against the idea. But – 'I know now that was the wrong advice.' She declined to go into the matter any further. It was nigh on impossible ever to extract any personal feedback about her family. Problems from the past were simply not worth dwelling on. It was the *now* that was important. Common sense again: only address matters if you can affect the outcome.

6 December 1953

PERSONAL POSER OF THE WEEK – THE LADY GETS A WINK FROM HER PAST

It's said that no woman marries the love of her life. All over the world, I suppose there are millions of women – most of them happily married – who indulge in the occasional good old brood over the love-that-might-have-been.

When, with shoes kicked off and work laid aside for a bit, they recall, with a pleasant melancholy, the most romantic moments of their lives, these memories are usually not of the men they married, but the men they nearly did.

THE PROBLEM

A sensible women will keep these memories as memories; but then a lot of women haven't a lot of sense. If the chance comes along to meet an old flame again, most women will take it, egged on by sentiment and curiosity, fifty-fifty.

A woman with just this problem wrote to me this week. She had been invited to lunch with a beau of twenty years ago, and she was making herself almost ill with indecision.

She believed her looks would stand up to the twenty-year gap.

'I still look young,' she writes. 'When I was twenty I looked thirty, and I have looked pretty much the same ever since.' Nor was there much of a moral problem, for her husband, amused, was urging her to go. On the other hand, she didn't want to go looking for trouble.

THE AUSPICES

What was she to do? Now I never set myself up as an adviser of affairs of the heart.

First, my advice is always terrible. Second, I have quite enough to do with running my own life.

And third, after you've talked to all your girlfriends, tossed up a coin and consulted the auspices, only one person can make up your mind for you – and that's you.

But I thought this problem of enough interest to give it some thought. I didn't come to a cut-and- dried conclusion, but here are some things to consider.

One: This meeting after a long gap is bound to unsettle you. One of two things will happen, and you'll be unsettled either way.

a) The man himself may not mean a button to you now. He may be bald and boring, and you may long for lunch to end. But you are still going to moon about the house for days afterwards, shedding a tear, not for *him*, but simply for the past.

b) He may *not* be bald and boring and you may *not* long for that lunch to be over. This is less likely, but it is just possible to pick up where you left off before, in which case you'll feel mad at the years you chucked away.

These are the arguments against going.

Two: There's a longish chance he may have changed so much that you will reach home with a shudder of relief. If he has grown mean-faced or grossly fat, you will feel quite drunk with your own good fortune, and you'll view your husband with a kindlier than usual eye.

Three: You'll spend days before your lunch sizing yourself up and getting yourself groomed.

You'll have your hair done, and a manicure, buy yourself a new suit. Whether you like him or not, you'll do your own ego a power of good.

These are the arguments in favour of going.

THE SOLUTION

I told you I hadn't any cut-and-dried solution. The pros and cons seem to work out about equal, and I'm not sure what the lady ought to do now.

But I do know what she should have done twenty years ago.

A relationship broken by a long gap is always a partial failure: instead of looking forward, it tends to look back. *She should never have let the friendship totally lapse.*

30 May 1954

THE TOPIC I'M SICK OF

Money, money, money. I'm tired of hearing about money. Nobody seems to talk about anything else. Have you noticed how *every* conversation – at a party, in a train, at the grocer's – veers round sooner or later to the eternal boring subject?

1. AT A DINNER PARTY
We started politely. With the soup and the fish, we ranged around Billy Graham, the Flower Show, Marlene Dietrich and Lord Beaverbrook.

But by the meat we'd got down to money.

The subdivision of the subject was income tax – how it doesn't pay to work, how nobody can build up a fortune any more, how you're handicapped if you haven't got capital, and how lucky people were who had a success before the war. We've said it all before. But that doesn't seem to stop us saying it all again.

2. ON A TRAIN TO OXFORD
I was talking to two young and pretty girls. We started talking about holiday clothes, about the things they'd bought and made for the summer, and about what they would need for a motor-coach holiday in Spain.

By the time we'd got to Reading we'd got on to money.

Holiday clothes led to holiday travel, and during the last part of the journey we thrashed out the currency problems of every country in Europe. We budgeted for imaginary holidays ranging from a month in Cyprus to two weeks in France with a tent, making detailed allowances for tips and something over to spend. Considerations of scenery, language, climate, architecture were submerged before the purely practical considerations of how much and how long.

TOO FRANK

Another symptom of the new money disease is the lack of good manners on the subject.

The pleasant convention that you didn't ask people how much they paid for things has given way to hideous frankness about prices and values.

'What did they rush you for that heavenly hat?' or 'What did you get for your house?' are now acceptable conversation.

Please don't think that in attacking all this money talk I acquit myself. I am absolutely fascinated by money. I too glorify what is largely money gossip by calling it economics.

I talk as much as anyone about tax, currency, Customs, price, salaries, wages, fares, subsidies, expenses, MPs' finances, authors' rights and the ghastly cost of living.

But I do think it is a boring thing to do. So if I stop it first, you stop it too. There are a million, million things better to say.

NOTES

Billy Graham (1918–2018) American evangelist who attracted massive crowds. Preached to 120,000 people at Wembley Stadium during his 'Great London Crusade' of 1954.

Marlene Dietrich (1901–1992) German-American actress, long-lasting glamour icon and sex symbol.

Lord Beaverbrook William Max Aitken, 1st Baron Beaverbrook (1879–1964) Newspaper publisher and owner of the *Daily Express* and the *Sunday Express*, the most successful mass-circulation newspapers in the world.

BEWARE THE VOICE OF THE VIPER

The saddest story of the week is the broken engagement of an invalid woman of forty-three and her fiancé of twenty-one.

'I can't stand friends visiting me,' said the lady in the case, 'because of the things they tell me are being said.'

My advice to that lady is: CHANGE YOUR FRIENDS. For 'I thought you should know' is the deadliest phrase in the English language. It is not the people who are talking about you who are doing the harm. The vipers are the people – who, meaning oh, so well – insist on telling you what other people say.

Broadly speaking, I am thoroughly in favour of gossip.

The vagaries of human nature provide half the fun in life, and it would be boring and unnatural to keep silent about them.

If the lady next door flirts outrageously with the milkman (heavily married) – I call that interesting and well worthy of comment.

If a film star is getting megalomania, or a prince loves a beggar maid or a City magnate is bursting for a peerage, or two MPs won't sit together, they are all providing legitimate topics of gossip.

After all there *are only* about five things to talk about: abstract ideas, the arts, daily life, places and people. Good conversation consists of a mixture of the elements, with a good whack of it spent on people.

Most of us talk a lot about our friends, and they talk about us. But we do not gossip to hurt them, and we do not love each other the less.

TALK THAT KILLS

BUT – the person who reports gossip to the subject of it – he is the mischief-maker. His is the talk that kills.

You can decently say 'Don't you think Harry's work is terrible lately?' That's fair comment (unless you say it to Harry's boss).

But: 'Harry, everyone is saying your work is terrible' is the voice of the viper. It raises mists of doubt in the wretched Harry's mind and he imagines that wherever people are gathering together, tongues are clacking to his detriment.

So, the lady-with-the-young fiancé, ignore your informative friends. If you want to be happy decide the issue on its merits.

If anyone says: 'I felt it was my duty to tell you', show that person the door.

15 May 1955

AM I WRONG TO WANT TO BE ALONE?

Something that ought to be free, but is becoming rarer than chinchilla – *privacy*. A bit of space to yourself will soon be a luxury that money can't buy.

TAKE A TAXI . . . and instead of dreaming happily away to yourself in the back you have to listen to a harsh, monotonous conversation between the driver and his radio headquarters.

'Forty-nine Grosvenor Square, forty-nine Grosvenor Square, forty-nine Grosvenor Square' – there's something fascist about it.

GO TO THE HAIRDRESSER . . . and instead of a nice, cosy cubicle, where you can really concentrate on *True Romances*, you sit at vast expense in a communal salon, moving at intervals from the chair to the basin, back to the chair, on to the drier, back to the chair, and so on. (I admit there is a certain charm in watching Lady A's hair being dipped at the roots, or listening to Mrs B and Mrs C discussing their love life

fortissimo under their driers. They forget that they can't hear, but everyone else can – clearly.)

WORK IN A BRAND NEW OFFICE . . . and instead of having a quiet room where you can do a day's work in a day you have a section of a smart sort of factory, where you spend the day mixing in with other people's phone conversations, and do the real work at home at night.

PLAN A NEW HOUSE . . . and the more you have to spend the more chance there is that your architect will build you one vast, handsome room divided loosely into different 'living units'. You know, one alcove for the super-kitchen, another for the super-baby, and so on.

Just as we get rid of over-crowding at one end of the social scale, up it comes at the other. Am I the last person in the world who likes to have my own little niche? If so, am I a psychological misfit? I'd like to know.

A PLAGUE ON ALL GIRLS WHO PLAY AT WORKING

I asked for tea and she brought me coffee 'SO sorry,' she said with a giggle. 'I never can remember who's ordered what.'

She was a waitress in a West End snack bar

* *

I asked the price of some dishes and if they were fireproof.

'I don't know the price exactly,' she said, 'but I expect it's labelled somewhere. I don't know if they are fireproof, but they don't *look* as if they'd crack.'

She was the salesgirl in the china and glass department.

* *

I asked about her shorthand typing.

'I'm afraid my typing is a bit rocky, but it ought to get better when I've had some practice. What time would I get away on Fridays? I'd like to catch the 5.15.'

She'd come to see me for a job.

* *

Goodness, how mad they make me, the nibblers at jobs, the dilettantes, the dabblers. The girls who want the money but can't be bothered to learn the technique. It's nice that today there is work for everyone and everyone works. But the pay-off is the battalions of amateurs who give half-baked service.

YOU FIND THEM

In shops . . . the girls who chat behind the counter while you wait for attention, who know less about the stock than you do

In offices . . . the girls who are always in the cloakroom making up.

In fashion . . . the girls who mess about as designers or dressmakers.

YOU FIND THEM

In catering . . . the girls who open soup kitchens or serve at coffee bars.

In interior decorating . . . because they have an eye for colour.

In the next few weeks, as the universities come down, as the schools break up, thousands of girls will start their first jobs. They'll be young – all the better. Inexperienced – doesn't matter.

But if they start with the amateur attitude they're doomed.

What makes a pro? I've collected opinions from some of the most famous employers in Britain.

Whitney Straight (deputy chairman of BOAC) 'A pro in our business is someone who can sink personal feelings. Our staff must take changes of schedule or rudeness of passengers in their stride.'

Edward Rayne (youngest chairman of a public company in Britain) 'The pro has a strong desire to earn money. The amateur reaches a certain salary level and makes no effort to earn that much more.'

Michael Joseph (the publisher) 'Our profession suffers terribly from amateurishness because everyone thinks he can write. But the pro writes and writes and writes until he can use words like precision tools.'

Hazel Hammond (managing director of two London stores) 'The pro has initiative and follows her work through from beginning to end. For instance, a good sales girl ties up with other departments. Having sold a dress, she suggests a new bag or a hat. The amateur sells a dress – maybe – and leaves it at that.'

NOTES

Whitney Willard Straight (1912-1979) Grand Prix motor racing driver with a passion for flying. He was born in New York, moving to England in 1925. After a life of glamour and daring-do, he became deputy chairman of BOAC in 1949.

Edward Rayne (1922-1992) Sir Edward Rayne was head of Rayne shoes. The company held royal warrants from both the Queen and the Queen Mother. Vivien Leigh, Ava Gardner and Rita Hayworth all wore Rayne. (My mother did not. She swore by Ferragamo, apparently the only European company with a truly 'slim fit'.)

Michael Joseph (1897-1958) Book publisher. Authors included H.E Bates, Monica Dickens, Vita Sackville-West. (My father, Macdonald Hastings, was to marry Michael Joseph's widow, Anthea Esther Hodson, in the 1960s.)

---

17 July 1955

CALLOUSNESS

I'm against capital punishment, but that's not the point. I feel a sympathy for desperate people, but that's nothing to do with it.

What shocked me most about the Ruth Ellis case was the callousness of ordinary people.

'A good riddance, I call it.'

'She did it, so she ought to hang.'

'If you live like that you must accept the consequences.'

Imagination, intelligence, charity seem to be submerged this week in self-righteousness. The nastiest trait in the British character.

NOTE

Ruth Ellis (1926–1955) Convicted of murdering her lover, she was the last woman to be hanged in Britain, at HM Prison Holloway in July 1955.

---

21 August 1955

CHARM – IS NOT ENOUGH

In the ordinary way, I'm no feminist. I think charm is a much better weapon for a woman to use than logic or efficiency.

But the Lime Grove attitude to women will soon turn me into a chained-to-the-railings suffragette. Agreed a woman on a TV fashion programme should be attractive. And models, announcers and entertainers should be pretty and chic.

But I do think that the women who discuss literature, history and public affairs (even on panel games) should have *some* intellectual capacity, even if it means a loss of glamour. Listening to the pretty nitwits airing their views on, say, Rousseau, sends shivers of humiliation down my spine, as they grope around trying to remember if he is dead or alive.

I refuse to believe there are *no* women who combine talking power with either good looks or strong personality.

How about Jacquetta Hawkes, Constance Cummings, Shirley Catlin, Enid Starkie, Elizabeth Pakenham, Dorothy Sayers?

NOTES

Jacquetta Hawkes (1910-1996) Archaeologist and writer.

Constance Cummings (1910-2005) Film and stage actress

Shirley Catlin Better known as Shirley Williams. A Labour MP 1964-79 and member of the Cabinet 1974-9, in 1981 she was one of the 'Gang of Four' rebels who founded the Social Democratic Party.

Enid Starkie (1897-1970) Literary critic, known especially for her biographical works on French poets.

Elizabeth Pakenham, Countess of Longford (1906-2002) Historian and biographer.

Dorothy Sayers (1893-1957) Crime writer and poet.

---

17 March 1957

HAVE YOU A COMMON STREAK?

It may be smarter than you think

Luckily for me, I have a very common streak. I don't mind in the least doing what everyone else does, if the idea is sound.

Now that mass production if so good and craftsmanship so bad, I find it pays to forget the snobberies of being 'individual' and to swim with the crowd.

This is specially true of clothes, holidays, and food.

Unless you are frightfully rich and can afford a yacht, Balenciaga, and a dish-to-order at Maxim's, it's best not to strain too hard for the personal touch.

This is the age of bulk planning and the machine. Better not to fight them – but to use them.

STARTING WITH CLOTHES
I am all for cheap, ready-made fashions, styled by top designers and turned out by the thousands.

I don't want my friends to give me any more addresses of marvellous little women.

I've *had* the little corsetières in mews, the little milliners in attics, and the little dressmakers who copy Paris models at high prices with a hundred fittings.

And I am equally sick of marvellous little men.

Of course, I admire the true craftsman, and a real couturier is worth his salt.

But good 'made - to - measure' is rare as diamonds and too many people are fatiguing amateurs.

GOING ON HOLIDAYS

. . . now nagging on our minds. I'm through with trying to get off the beaten track. There are so many beaten tracks that the only places where you can really be on your own are a desert, a mud flat, the cold side of a mountain, or a tundra region out of season.

PARIS FOR ME

I'd sooner settle for something as well trodden as Paris in the spring, or summer in Capri.

The individualists say go to the offbeat places, or to the beauty spots out of season. But this is surely the way to miss all the wonders of the world.

What's the point of going to the only Devon village without any thatch or the only Greek island without any ruins? Or to Rome in the rain?

AND AS FOR FOOD

I've no time any more for the quaint little restaurants where they pluck the bamboo shoots before your very eyes.

Or (as happened to me once) to glimpse through the bead curtain an Arab boy straining my coffee though his sock.

Do you know where to get the quickest meal in London? Roast beef, French salad, and a glass of wine?

Served to the tune of a thousand meals a day in That Corner House.

NOTE

'That Corner House' – Lyons Corner Houses were huge restaurants that featured large throughout the thirties, forties and fifties. Mother favoured The Seven Stars, in Coventry Street, Piccadilly, and we went for treats. Roast beef was the order of the day. I thought it the height of sophistication. My father's career kick-started in Lyons' public relations.

---

26 July 1957

BE CALM – OR TRY TO BE

Always ready (too ready) to offer good advice. Auntie Scott-James will now give you one simple rule on how to move house. The one thing is to wrap yourself for the day in a yogi calm.

I got into a remote, abstracted mood at eight o'clock on the fatal morning.

IT SURVIVED the moment when a crate of clocks and china hurtled three storeys down the lift shaft.

IT SURVIVED the moment when eight men said they felt like a strong cup of tea and the cooker was still at the back of the van.

IT SURVIVED the moment when they told me the drawing room floorboards would have to come up – and my lovely new lilac carpet had been laid the day before.

BUT IT BROKE when I crawled into bed at night to relax with a French novel and found that all the books were in boxes in the attic except three loose ones. They were called *With Shield and Assegai, Son of a Gun, and Minor Tactics of the Chalk Stream*.

I made a noisy fuss.

MY DREAM – IS IT POSSIBLE?

I had a dream that:

* I caught a plane without having to get up at half-past six.
* I went to the cinema and the nearest person eating chocs was five rows away.
* I bought some foundation cream and it came out the same colour as last time.
* I read an American fashion magazine without feeling terribly discontented (why *should* I have to rub along without a satin trench coat?).
* I lived somewhere where it was technically impossible to fix a TV or a telephone.
* I took my children to the Park without someone threatening to report me to the NSPCC.

4 August 1957

JAMBOREE – YOUR VIEW?

What's your opinion of the Boy Scouts? This week they celebrate their Jubilee Jamboree, and the streets are full of men in Scout kit. You never saw so many neckerchiefs, badges, lanyards and knobbly knees.

I find the subject is violently controversial. I am surprised that people feel so strongly.

Hero-worship

Many parents object to a movement which springs from the old days of flag-waving, whose moral code is smug, and which makes a fetish of hero-worship and uniforms.

Others say the movement is entirely sound. Its ideals are fine, it gives the boys plenty of practical things to do, and it gets them out into the fresh air.

My own feeling is one of surprise that an organization which seems so old-fashioned should actually be gaining ground every year.

The Scout movement is frankly rooted in the Boer War

The uniform is 'very like the uniform worn by the men of the South African Constabulary' (I quote from the Scouts' handbook).

The Scouts' chorus is a 'chant that the African Zulus used to sing to their chief. It may be shouted on the march, or used as applause at games and meetings and camp fires.'

The Scouts' staff is 'an invaluable assistant when traversing mountains or boulder-strewn country, and especially in night work in forest or bush'.

It's Victorian.

And the moral code is essentially Victorian. For instance, a strong reason for learning tracking is so that you can hunt down a servant when he steals your property.

Tracking is also useful for catching a pig in prickly cactus country, or for rounding up a stolen camel.

I am afraid that very few of a Scout's accomplishments seem to me to be useful for everyday modern life. Personally I can never think of anything for them to do in bob-a-job week.

It worries me so much that I have to go round the house creating jobs.

But if boys (and men) like to escape the jet age and pretend to be Empire builders, explorers, and pioneers, I don't see that they can do much harm.

Do you?

My father, Macdonald Hastings,
tooling up.

Anne and Men

There is no doubt that Anne preferred the company of men to that of most women, so she fitted well into the male-dominated world of Fleet Street. In 2007, when she featured on *Desert Island Discs*, she recalled it as a 'heavenly' place to work. The newspapers nestled cheek by jowl, and the bars and restaurants heaved with columnists from every paper. Just walking down the street guaranteed a social encounter.

In 1953, when she first took up her desk at the *Sunday Express*, it was not fellow journalists who objected to their new columnist, but the men in the print union. Anne was a woman, and women were simply not allowed 'on the stone' ('the stone' was where the type was set into layout format and page proofs pulled off for last-minute changes and corrections prior to publication). All her male colleagues went down to the stone to check their copy. Anne could not. Back in 1953 the factory floor felt that women should 'know their place'.

Eventually, after much cajoling, there was a moment when she was allowed down, really as a token gesture. Hands were solemnly shaken, a point was made and a tradition broken – but for all that, she never went back on the stone during the rest of her time at the *Express*, or later on the *Mail*.

Anne relished being a woman in a man's world. She certainly didn't class herself as a feminist. Men and women were to be treated equally, your gender immaterial. Employment should always be based on your merit, not your sex. She hated the idea of any government recommendation that aimed to boost women in the workplace or skew statistics. We were quite capable of getting where we wanted under our own steam. Anne also felt that women were the stronger sex mentally, better at coping with life's myriad disasters without crumbling, and they didn't need to be patronized by politicians.

In her personal life, Anne was obviously never going to attract a partner who suffered from insecurity. She was highly independent and used to running the show. Anne was in no sense of the word 'needy', and she looked for a husband who would share her interests in books, the arts, and travel. She also enjoyed sex. Over the years she made some errors in choice, but she never talked down her previous partners. She knew that no harm had been intended – they had just met at the wrong time, in the wrong circumstances, or were simply Incompatible.

Anne married three times. Her first husband, Derek Verschoyle, was the literary editor of *The Spectator*. They married in 1939, and were together for months rather than years. She never mentioned him to me. She said after they divorced it was as if they 'had never been'. Ships in the night.

Mother met my father, Macdonald Hastings, during her time on *Picture Post*. He was tall and dashing and their war correspondent. He too had been married before. She had hoped his interests would include the family, holidays, gardening and a shared love of the countryside. She was right about the gardening (although it was vegetables, not flowers, that really excited him). As for the rest, her mind had clearly been elsewhere when she agreed to marry him. This was a man who was in 1953 writing for the children's comic *Eagle*. He was '*Eagle*'s Special Investigator' and entertained a generation of children with his tales of daring-do – 'How I Became a Snake Charmer', 'Riding the Cresta Run', 'A Knife Thrower's Target' are all samples of the weekly thrills that Mac attempted and endured in order to entertain his young readers. He was a fan of hunting, shooting and fishing, which stood him in good stead when he went on to appear on the *Tonight* programme reporting on the countryside. But none of this amused Anne. She was appalled by his cavalier attitude to firearms, and his lack of interest in anything of a cerebral or arty nature. This was a woman who preferred picking wild flowers to picking up pheasants. They were married for eighteen years, but their respective journalistic careers meant that when things were dire they didn't have to spend much time in the same house.

I saw so little of my father, that the times he was there remain quite memorable occasions. My parents never seemed to row in my presence either. Obviously there were a couple of interesting set-to's, usually involving my brother and some gun crisis or other (my father was not familiar with gun safety precautions), and, although I was too young to be very aware, the political crisis over Suez apparently caused meltdown. Mac was very right-wing, Anne a liberal, so politically they were poles apart. Mac saw the Suez venture as a blow struck for England, and Anthony Eden as the hero of the hour. Mother saw it as an act of barbarism. As she later said, 'After Suez we never looked the same way again.' They had, however, worked out their own personal modus operandi, and I cannot say that when the divorce came it caused me any great emotional disturbance. My parents just lived in separate houses.

She remained fond of him. Anne cried very rarely, but far from cheering when the divorce papers came through she was

Anne's brother, John.

miserable. Similarly, after his funeral she rang me and sobbed down the phone.

Her height played a part in her relationship with men. She said it was always expected that she would drive the car and carry the suitcases. Anne was a very fast walker, and could always be seen striding ahead on any ramble, the man in her life several yards behind. Her practical capability had started in her own youth. Her brother, John, was epileptic, and it had fallen on Anne to be his principal carer and friend. This was not a hardship, for she adored him. If she wasn't at school she would be looking after John. Her time at Oxford was the only period when she couldn't be there for him. As soon as she went on to her job on *Vogue*, she once more took up her role as his friend and companion: he was the 'best friend and ally I ever had'.

Anne was not interested in protestations of love.

Expressions of a man's love never move me as much as even the smallest act of kindness. In the course of my life many men have told me they loved me, but after the excitement of the beginning I don't find much meaning in it. A man's 'I love you' usually means 'I need you', 'I want you to do things for me.' But the man who brings you a cup of tea when you are tired, or suggests a holiday, or discusses the children with you on a serious, not perfunctory, level is the one who really loves you. Of course, if I were honest, the kind men I have known have been extremely boring. Perhaps to be interesting a man has to be more interested in other things (his work, or the arts) than the woman in his life.

Mother described Osbert as a 'slightly above average selfish person'. But he was also the love of her life. She adored him. They shared the same interest in everything. In their attitudes to gossip, books, music, travel, food, humour, they were completely compatible. They might well be the last generation to have written love letters. Whenever they were apart they sent letters to each other on a daily basis. Our loss that emails and texts have taken the drama out of this simple, elegant way of transmitting affection. Their marriage was one of extreme happiness for only eight years. Then he suffered a stroke, after which nothing was quite the same. He could still draw, and go out to his clubs and to dinner, but his capacity slowly diminished and with it his good temper, which faded through frustration. But she never complained about this change to his previous exuberant personality.

When Osbert died, after his long and debilitating illness, Anne took up letter-writing again. For a year she filled page after page with letters to Osbert, letting him know who she had seen, what she had done and how much she missed him. 'Last night I dreamed you were telephoning me from New York, and I heard your voice quite loud and clear, the sound waking me up: "Darling, it's Osbert" – if only I could have retreated back into my dream and heard some more. Have I ever explained that the cord that binds us is a strong as ever? But I CAN cope.'

Even in the throes of misery, Anne's inner strength came through. She accepted life's blows with extraordinary fortitude, part of her 'we weren't put on this earth to have fun' philosophy. But she remained after Osbert's death 'half the person ever since'.

4 September 1955

ROMANTIC – AND WRONG

My husband, like all good Englishmen and true, is convinced that the Mediterranean is not only a haunt of vice, a breeding ground for mosquitoes, and a hotbed of discomfort and disease, but that it also has a climate far inferior to our own.

To confirm this, he has fixed our outdoor thermometer on the wall of the house next to the boiler.

All through the summer he has proved to his own satisfaction (though not to mine) that our garden has been hotter than Rome, Cairo or Madrid.

By clever stoking he will keep the temperature up in the seventies till the end of September, and will be sitting outside long after he has caught his first cold.

What dreamy romantics Englishmen are.

I HAVE NEVER BEEN KISSED ON THE TOES

As you know, I have never set up to be a counsellor on affairs of the heart – my advice would be quite disastrous.

But I bet I know a thing or two more than two American experts who have just published a book called *Marriage Manners*.

Any wife who followed their advice would, I maintain, be a natural for the divorce court. No man could stand such calculated coyness for more then the statutory three years.

'**DON'T** be afraid of enthusiasm. Rave about the job Bob did whitewashing the cellar. Exclaim over the first wisps of grass. Make your eyes sparkle, and love the whole wonderful act of living.'

'**IF** he starts sniffing suspiciously when you try out a new dinner dish, explain: "Here's a dish I learned to make in cooking class, and as a meat substitute it's a real food bill saver."'

'**BLEND** laughter with love at every opportunity – like sending your darling half a dozen birthday cards signed by movie stars.'

'**JOIN** your husband as he jokes or pokes fun at you. He's not jesting with any old person. You're on his team – remember?'

'**MASTER** the art of listening. When your husband speaks, give him the benefit of your undivided attention.'

'**IF** you go to a party where your husband has old friends but you know no one, and he drifts off and leaves you alone, don't sit in injured solitude. Say "Hi" to the gang around you and start making your own knot of friends.'

Well, I don't know about you, but if I sent my darling a lot of birthday cards signed by movie stars he'd think I needed psychoanalysing, and if I said 'Hi' to the gang around me at a party he'd think it was time to go home.

The authors round off all this lunatic advice with a rich touch of snobbery.

'**MARRIAGE** is all the nice things you ever wanted: the place of your own, the bone china, the crystal goblets, the silverware, the candlelight, the buffet supper. It's looking ahead and saving for things, the thrill of a bright, white washing machine . . . It's the raise you celebrate, the furniture you refinish, the kiss that tingles the end of your toes.'

Again, I'm afraid that none of this goes for me.

Our goblets were smashed long ago, I'm not too sure that our china is bone, and (I hate to admit it), I've never been kissed on the toes.

18 December 1955

I KNOW WHAT MAKES TIRED BUSINESS-MEN TIRED

All over this great commercial land of ours are dear, kind business wives worrying themselves to death because their husbands work too hard.

'Henry's dead beat when he gets home,' they say . . . 'Henry's business is taxing his strength . . .' Henry is doing too much.'

I got to worrying about Henry myself. Just what does Henry *do* that makes him look such a wreck when he gets home?

I understand what doctors do, and what actors do, and what farmers do, and milkmen and miners do. But none of them are so tired as Henry. Making the business wheels go round must be very hard labour.

Well, I've been looking into it. I've been looking at the lives of some tired gentlemen in the directing, managing and executive world.

And I've come to the conclusion that what's killing them is their lunch.

They are fresh and cheerful before this event, exhausted and stertorous after it.

I started in the City . . . with the bankers and brokers and promoters who make copper go up and mines go down..

They get to the office about 9.30 and spend a quiet morning till 11.30 or 12.00 studying the market and dictating and phoning a bit. Nothing gruelling so far – they've used up less units of energy than their wives back at home.

But at noon they enter into shocking conditions of work, which any strong union would condemn. These poor fellows have to put in three hours of continuous work, *most standing up,* in hot, smoky, underground bars. For it's an unwritten business rule that no big deal can be put through except over drinks or a heavy lunch.

I went to one of the City restaurant-bars where commerce hums. I saw what looked like groups of men enjoying double gins.

But I'd got it all wrong. These men were not enjoying themselves. They were hard at work.

I asked about a puce-faced gentlemen who was knocking back doubles in a corner. 'That's Sir Charles,' they told me. 'He's negotiating a sticky million-pound deal.'

'What about Foxy-Face over by the bar?' I asked. 'I suppose Oils would collapse and the widows and orphans would be ruined if he didn't stand the fat man another Scotch?'

'He's a very big accountant,' they said 'and it so happens he's had a very useful morning. He's been hard at it since noon.'

By three o'clock they all looked done in. What with the drinks and the heat and the smoke and the shellfish and the chops and steaks and cheese, they looked years older than the alert fellows who had entered.

This week executives everywhere are being tortured by the abundance of Christmas parties. **It seems that every businessman in every business must somehow manage to see every other businessman he knows between now and Christmas.**

You see, it's all a question of good will. It also seems that no firm can hold up its head unless it gives a Christmas party.

Such a load of obligations keeps the businessman wassailing until well into the evening.

'Simply must show my face at the Industrial Glove party – they like me to come.'

'I daren't cut the Tomkins and Tomkins show – they're biggish clients.'

'Must have a little get-together with the other chaps on Friday – they'd appreciate it.'

Poor Henry is in for a frightfully tiring week.

12 March 1956

YOUR HUSBAND – DON'T GRUMBLE

Do you ever grumble, even in the smallest degree, about your husband? Such as wishing he would notice the ashtrays or be more helpful with the washing-up? You don't realize how lucky you are.

THINK of Mrs Mortimer Leigh, happily married for thirty-three years, who discovered the other day that Mr Leigh had had another happy 'wife' and family for sixteen years only two miles away.

THINK of Mrs Janis of Chicago, whose husband locked her in the house when he went to the office and nipped back several times a day to make sure she hadn't found a way out.

THINK of Mrs Thomas of New York, who scraped and scrubbed all her life on so little that the children's clothes were ragged, and has just discovered, at the age of sixty, that her husband has been a millionaire all the time.

THINK of the wife in Copenhagen whose husband got so mad when she squeezed the toothpaste from the middle instead of the end that he knocked her out with her own hot water bottle.

THINK of Mrs Grigg in the north country, whose husband was so crazy for sausages and mash that he ate them for every meal for seventeen years and none of the family were allowed a different dish.

See what I mean about *your* husband? Doesn't he seem wise, kind, tolerant, gentle and generous by comparison?

29 July 1956

I KNOW IT'S A WICKED QUESTION . . . BUT WOULD YOU DO ALL THIS FOR A MAN?

Would *you* do as much for a man as Marilyn Monroe?

I've never met the lady and I've only seen one Monroe film, and it wasn't very special. But the Monroe charm and guts that have bowled over Milton Shulman and Sir Laurence Olivier and Edith Sitwell and Terence Rattigan are beginning to get to me too.

Quite a lot of trouble is coming to that girl. Or perhaps it won't come, but she's taking the risk with her great blue eyes wide open.

Now she's going to marry Arthur Miller, she is going to run up against the Un-American Activities people, and the American Legion, and the powerful reactionary American women's clubs, and the Daughters of the American Revolution who nearly did for Ingrid Bergman.

She's going to read plenty of cracks like the one that appeared last week in a big Hollywood column: She's the girl that likes Commies.

THE ODDS AGAINST

She may make bigger and better pictures, yet see their box office takings go down.

At the best, she will hear her husband referred to as an 'egg-head' – which means he's got brains. At the worst she may see him spend a year in jail.

When she has embraced the Jewish faith, she will be barred from many of the smartest places and functions in America. (I once went to a ball on Long Island and was told; 'You are now entering a house where no Jew has ever set foot.')

All this is pretty solemn thinking for the prettiest blonde in the business, who is accustomed to more adulation than all the other pin-ups put together.

I would like to think that Marilyn was the one witch the witch-hunters couldn't catch, but the odds are against her.

HOW MANY WOMEN WOULD DO THE SAME?

30 June 1957

MAD DOGS AND . . .

Up goes the thermometer, and the Englishman goes berserk. The rich strain of insanity that built us the Empire in the hottest spots of the world drives us to startling (if totally unnecessary) feats of endurance.

WHY do families pull up to picnic within three feet of the hottest, dustiest, fastest, noisiest bypass they can find? I am always astonished to see family parties with children in crawlers, a frail old granny and a couple of dogs, eating their lunch within the slipstream of a thousand cars an hour. You'd think they'd turn up some shady lane . . . but no. They like to be as near as possible to other picnic parties and other cars.

WHY do cyclists, bent over the wheel and backs turned towards the sun, travel stripped to the waist? I shudder for them as I see the raw, red flesh, the peeling skin, and imagine the burning pain they are going to suffer at night.

WHY do we pull back the curtains and open the windows, ignoring the experience of all the southerners that closed, covered windows keep a room cool?

AND WHY do men keep to their idiotic dress conventions? Choked at the neck, tight at the waist and wrapped in 100 per cent pure Yorkshire worsted, the Englishman in a heatwave is a symbol of courage – but he may look a bit of an ass.

4 August 1957

WHY BE SHOCKED WHEN GIRLS CHOOSE HUSBANDS OVER FIFTY?

I can't think why anyone's surprised at Ethel Drew (a winsome twenty-five) marrying Wilfrid Hyde-White (a quizzical fifty-four). I can't think why anyone's shocked at Audrey Hepburn (an elfin twenty-seven) marrying Mel Ferrer (a thrice-married forty), and playing opposite Fred Astaire (fifty-seven) in *Funny Face* and now Gary Cooper (fifty-six) in *Love in the Afternoon*. I can't think why anyone should squawk at Kay Kendall (a ravishing thirty) going for Rex Harrison (a somewhat beaten-up fifty).

Just a schoolboy
Anyone with a gleam of intelligence can see that all the poor girls are trying to do is to ensure that they marry a grown-up man. Because one of the most disheartening things in a woman's life is discovering, as she grows older, that all men are just gweat big gwown-up school-boys.

When you're eighteen you dream of marrying a terribly mature man of twenty-eight or thirty, who'll know all about life and be much wiser than you are. You soon learn that a man of twenty-eight is about as mature as Billy Bunter.

When you're twenty-five you cast a hopeful eye on the man of forty, who has knocked about the world and is at the top of his profession. By now, he ought to know *something* about *something*.

He's tactless
But you soon learn that the man who is a magnetic speaker in the House of Commons or holds the

scales of life or death in the operating theatre is still, in private life, Smith Minor of the Upper Fourth.

Tactless with relatives, childish over a new motor car, petulant if baulked of a treat, and fussy as a baby if he cuts his finger or catches a cold.

By the time you are thirty-five or forty you settle, against your will, for being a matriarch, ruling the roost, holding all the affairs of the family in the hollow of your hand.

Most women adapt to this readily enough, treating their husbands as indulgently as an extra son.

They smile as they tell you 'My husband is a terror for playing with the children's toys.' Or 'The boys have gone off together for the day', one boy being Nicky, a leggy youth of sixteen, and the other being Henry, a heavy-breathing lad of forty-five.

But you get the odd woman who can't take it
Who thinks if she marries a much, much older man, she'll get an adult.

Well, I hope Ethel Drew, Audrey Hepburn and Kay Kendall won't be disappointed.

And I hope Valerie Fletcher (thirty), who has married T.S. Eliot (sixty-eight), doesn't find him terribly immature.

And I hope Mrs Hillstrom (forty-one), who has just married Nobel Prizewinner Sir Robert Robinson (seventy), doesn't find he's just another lovable schoolboy.

I know who *I*'d choose if I were marrying again, and it would be Bertrand Russell (eighty-five), who seems to me always charming, brilliant and wise.

And if he turned out to be boorish and unsophisticated, do you know what I'd do? I'd go back to playing with dolls.

NOTES

Wilfrid Hyde-White (1903–1991) English character actor. More a question of what wasn't he in. Married twice. Ethel Drew was his second wife.

---

11 August 1957

MEN ARE SO AWFUL IN BOATS – BUT I'LL SAIL AGAIN

The only time in my life when I did a lot of sailing was twenty years ago, when I fell in love with a young man with a boat. It was a great relief to me when I fell out of love with him and switched to a young man with a nice little car.

I used to be sick when it was rough, and impatient when it was calm, and cold and cross when we got stuck on sandbanks.

The other thing I have against sailing is that men become so *awful* when they are in charge of a boat.

I have been sworn at by men who are gentle to a fault in ordinary life . . . shouted at by timid intellectuals . . . bawled at by bossy mariners who wouldn't say boo to the office boy on dry land.

But I see I've got to take to sea again, Because sailing is becoming such a fashionable sport that I shall be left out by the tide if I can't do it.

Every season new yacht clubs spring up, and thousands of beginners take to the boats. Even reservoirs and flooded gravel pits are dotted with neat dinghies at weekends.

IN FAVOUR – better pills

I must admit that a sailing boat is such a delicious sight, and seasickness pills have reached such a peak of efficiency, that I want to have a go again. Even I can see great points in favour.

- Sailing is heaven for children. It makes them feel adventurous and useful. There is the thrill of the occasional fright, and the exhilarating sense of accomplishment as each piece of new technique is learned.
- Women say it makes their weekends a real holiday, instead of a time for extra work. 'I used to do all the cooking and chores for six of us,' one woman told me. 'Now we all pack off to our boat in Bosham, and the work is naturally shared. It isn't work anyway – it's just a picnic.'

You can see, the children have been getting at me. They've even taken me to a local regatta.

I have an ugly feeling that this may be the last summer when I shall sleep in a well-sprung bed. Next sailing season, I'll be curling up in a something bunk.

22 September 1957

CONSIDER: WOULD YOU MARRY AGAIN?

Take your eyes from this newspaper for a minute, Mr Jones, stare at the ceiling, and ask yourself a poignant question.

If you fell *under* the 8.15 train tomorrow morning, instead of stepping *into* it, would your wife marry again?

Since the Pope's statement that it may be better for a widow not to remarry, all the deep problems of widowhood, not often discussed, have exploded to the surface.

Women everywhere are asking themselves secretly, 'What would I do if it happened to me?'

Your first snap judgement, Mr Jones, may tell you that your wife has been so happy with you, she won't want to marry again. She will live on memories of her marriage, keeping everything just like *you* kept it . . . doing things the way *you* liked them. She will be critical of other men, because they won't come up to *your* standard.

But I think your snap judgement is wrong. The widow of a truly happy marriage is the one most likely to marry again.

She is good at marriage. She enjoys marriage. And she believes that her first husband, having truly loved her, will understand and approve if she chooses a second.

I found in talking to many women that none of them felt the slightest guilt towards their first husbands. They were sure that John . . . Jack . . . Peter . . . Henry would have wanted it. So would Humphrey Bogart, happily married for twelve years to Lauren Bacall, who says frankly: 'I hate being single. I am not one of those emancipated women who like to live alone.'

Mme Suzy Volterra, the lovely French widow, has told me exactly the same thing.

'Whenever I read that a man has expressed a wish in his will that his dear wife shall not remarry, I always think: I bet that man was a pig of a husband, and led her a horrible life. No loving husband would want his wife to be lonely.'

So when you ask yourself, Mr Jones, if your wife would remarry if you fell under the train, there's no need to feel self-satisfied if the answer if 'No'.

If the answer is 'Yes', it may well be that you've done her proud.

NOTE
Mme Suzy Volterra (1912–2006) Celebrated French racehorse owner.

THE TRUTH ABOUT HUSBANDS

Yet another wife has discovered one of the universal truths. 'Wilfrid', says Mrs Hyde-White, 'is just like a little boy.' The fact is that that Ethel Hyde-White – a lovely auburn-haired American girl of twenty-six – is mothering that witty husband of hers (aged fifty-four) as though he were a merry, precocious child. He has just had Asian flu.

'Was he a good patient?' I asked her.

She smiled indulgently. 'Well, when he was bad he moaned all day, and insisted on a great many pills. But he was very brave when he got better. I'm taking great care of him now because he's a bit chesty.'

He's changed . . .

I asked her who had had to do the adjusting to bridge the age gap in their marriage.

'We get on so well', she said 'that there wasn't much to do. But Wilfrid has changed a good deal. He's much tidier. Much more thoughtful. And so much happier than when I first met him.'

Mrs Hyde-White is busy furnishing their new flat.

'Wilfrid leaves all the choosing to me,' she said. 'In fact, it was only when I'd bought a lot of green furniture that he mentioned that he doesn't like green. But it will be quite easy to cover it all with slip covers.'

Calm, confident and almost maternal, Mrs Hyde-White confirms my old contention that the clinging little wife is a non-existent myth.

However young a woman is when she marries, give her a couple of weeks and she's in charge.

My father at the cottage, with a flintlock pistol.
At this point he clearly had a shoe shelf, and was
allowed to display his ship in a bottle.

Anne's bedroom in Rose Cottage, complete with her favourite interior features, a fire and a basin.

Anne and Interior Decoration

Anne's style of decoration was 'the poor woman's version of John Fowler' (her words, not mine). The decorator she admired beyond all other. When she first saw his work in country houses during the 1930s, she was 'bowled over by their beauty'. She loved the countrified atmosphere of his rooms, and set about trying to emulate it. In 1938, borrowing the money from her mother, she purchased at auction a small, dilapidated, doll's house of a cottage on the Berkshire downs. A home she literally fell in love with. Throughout her life the cottage and its garden were a constant source of pride and solace.

The rooms were painted white, a local carpenter laid an oak floor and Anne's Singer sewing machine was put to good use making curtains and dressing table frills in striped chintz and muslin. Her pride and joy was a painted dining room table – the real McCoy – bought from the actual Colefax & Fowler shop (oh, joy!) for £15. It was white, with a border painted apple-green on the top, the fat turned legs also picked out in apple-green. This table remained a firm favourite and was one of the few pieces of furniture to make the move to London when the cottage was eventually sold.

Anne picked up other pieces of furniture at local auctions and bric-a-brac shops. The dining chairs had ivy-print fabric on the backs and a Regency chaise longue was a feature, with a curved wooden dragon carving, his teeth, eyes and scales picked out in the table's green and white (I think this embellishment may have been added by Mother, as the technique was not up to Fowler standards), and initially covered in a yellow-and-white-striped satin. There were low built-in bookshelves on one side of the room, with a couple of cupboards to house in equal measure alcohol and board games, while the top shelf was used to display her other great love, which was porcelain.

She had inherited quite a good collection, and those flowery plates that weren't on shelves were hooked to the wall, alongside wood mirrors, the frames invariably painted à la Fowler. Mother's practical nature could also be seen in the cottage. There was only one bathroom, so a basin was put into each room to avoid a queue. Her colour of choice for upholstery was usually a rather yellowy green, and there were accents of pink in the china and cushions. The green colour followed me through childhood. I developed quite an aversion to it, although recently

I have come round to it, and rather long to re-cover a sofa. Anne would be delighted.

Flowers were in every room and, while admiring the Constance Spry form of arranging, Anne disliked what she would call 'shop' flowers. She loved the pick-and-mix nature of a cottage vase, and the car was regularly filled with bunches wrapped in newspaper to transport up to town.

Unlike a lot of homes in the fifties, ours were warm. In London we lived in a serviced block, huge boilers pumping up heat from the basement. In the cottage there were small bar electric fires sunk flat into the walls. One per room giving off quite a lot of heat and a cheery glow. You could make toast in front of them, as long as you were careful not to let the metal prongs of the fork touch the bars. Mother was a huge fan of the portable version too, bemoaning its eventual demise. Apparently, *proper* country houses were heated with these. Blow heaters when they appeared were not considered satisfactory. You needed to see the heat. There was also an open fire in the sitting room.

The cottage kitchen initially had a Rayburn range fuelled with coke, which was a bit of a faff, but once going sent out buckets of heat, and we always had lots of hot water. All our beds were equipped with hot water bottles. Mother really rated comfort, and did not believe in the idea of just putting on another jumper. She liked a nice cosy house.

Apart from the early days in the cottage, when necessity played a part, Anne did not tackle general decoration. A man was brought in. Mother belonged to the old school of redecoration, which believed there should be little – if possible, no – disruption to self. Nothing was put away or removed from the room except by the decorator. Preferably it should be completed within the week, all items cleaned, dusted and returned to their set place. This must have placed quite a lot of stress on the average painter, especially when it came to putting the breakables out of harm's way, but that was the approved method.

Anne certainly believed that a bath was for life, and would have made short shrift of the current vogue for replacing them on a whim. The same went for kitchens. Once completed a redesign of these rooms was actively disapproved of. A new cooker maybe, a fridge if the old one had died, but that was it. Anything else, a waste of money. My own home projects had to be planned with clandestine care to avoid recriminations.

Anne wrote a lot of pieces on the home. It was a subject that fascinated her. She certainly didn't trust machines or gadgets and always adopted them years after everyone else had installed them as standard. It took a lot of persuasion to encourage her to buy a washer-dryer, a dishwasher, or any sort of blender. She said she was nervous of them, and of course while she had the staff to complete these tasks by hand she really had no need for them. Later, as help diminished, she was forced to adopt them, but the myriad buttons and programmes were a source of angst.

Anne was not a trendsetter, but she had access to the designers and people who were, and, of course, she was a quick learner. She was a huge admirer of Terence Conran but, although she rather fancied the idea of a modern house, would never have made the leap required to turn his designs into reality.

Osbert brought a theatrical flair to his design of rooms. When we moved in, his drawing room was already a set piece. Dark green walls, red curtains, and a gold star wallpaper twinkling on the ceiling. It was a treat, and Anne didn't feel any need to change it. Indeed, further down the line when they moved, it was reproduced so exactly that Osbert could hardly have known they had changed location.

Over the years the cottage was extended, first to accommodate us children, and later adding on a small studio room for Osbert, complete with an oriel window which fitted his drawing desk and materials. Although Anne accepted the need for the alterations, her preference was always for the original – just as it had been when she first spotted it, half hidden by the ancient apple trees. A tiny, square, red-brick dolls' house, that for over sixty years she called home.

Anne's dressing table in Rose Cottage.
Every jar in order.

22 January 1956

CHILLY?

'The English country house in winter', said Count von Rumford in 1800, 'is the smallest in the civilized world – 25 square feet.'

He referred to the small habit - able area around the fire.

The years between have done little to warm things up.

The century and a half that has given us the joys of the steam engine, the airplane, equal franchise, synthetic fibres, trade unions and the atom bomb have left us as frozen as we were before (*the only new crumb of comfort is the electric blanket*). Indoor life in England is almost unbearable from November to March.

How's your dining room, for instance? Snug and hospitable ... or do you regularly apologise to your guests with the fateful words 'I'm afraid it's rather cold in here', spoken each time with fresh surprise?

How's your bathroom? Mine's like a morgue, with steam condensing in rivers on the walls. But the one room where you are both wet and naked at the same time should surely be caressingly warm.

How's your bedroom? Is it a pleasure to change into evening dress for a party ... or do you peel off each layer of day with a shudder.

How are your weekends? Do you look forward to an invitation to a country house? I dread the things. The only country friends I know whose homes are warm are Americans, who manage to jack the air up to a temperature that can support human life. We live under the romantic delusion that Nature has blessed us with a Gulf Stream which makes our climate muggy and mild. So our houses are badly built, badly warmed and badly insulated. The best modern houses have fires built out, or even in the middle of the room. There is more space round the fire and no heat is wasted.

NOTE
Sir Benjamin Thompson, Count von Rumford (1753-1814), an Anglo-American scientist; and inventor of among other useful objects, the Rumford fireplace.

I SAY, SCRAP YOUR DINING ROOM

I've got my eye on a major change in the structure of the English house. The *separate dining room is disappearing*. I'll take a small bet that in twenty years time, the dining room will be as obsolete as the still room is today.

There are plenty of sound reasons why the dining room is going out of business.

As help gets scarcer, you want to cut the labour of moving food from the place where it's cooked to the place where it's eaten.

As more women take jobs and more children lunch at school, the dining room is so under-worked it isn't worth having. It looks un-lived in and cheerless and is always 10 degrees colder than the rest of the house.

As homes get smaller, we need to use the space as sensibly as we can. For instance, I believe most families would find a play room twice as useful as a dining room.

I want to scrap our own dining room and turn it into a room where the children can set up their games and leave them undisturbed.

All right we've killed the dining room – so where do we eat?

THE BAR – and kitchen

An actress acquaintance has used an American idea. There is a bar (or counter) at one end of a large sitting room, with a kitchen unit behind it. From this she dispenses delicious light suppers to her guests, who sit on stools. She says this is ideal for entertaining at short notice, which is the kind of party she likes best. But there is also an alcove for ordinary sit-down suppers.

Another friend, who has just got engaged, has scrapped his dining room – he thinks they are stuffy and dreary – 'a room should be for moving and doing.' In his basement he has a low round table near the window with banquettes to sit on, and a roasting spit and charcoal grill in the middle of the room, where he cooks himself.

I have seen a Regency dining room divided from the very modern kitchen part by a marble counter and two-way cupboards.

You don't have to live in an engine-turned house made of glass, aluminium or laminated something or other. Whether your taste is ancient or modern, the combining of cooking and eating makes perfect sense.

22 July 1956

ARTIST WITH AN EYE ON THE WORLD

What a pleasure to meet an artist who does not despise the ways of the world.

I spent an afternoon with Fornasetti of Milan, formerly a painter and sculptor, now acknowledged as one of the best living designers of furniture and pottery.

'My aim', Fornasetti told me, 'is to bring as much imagination as possible to the most ordinary household things. Most modern artists only want to paint easel pictures. If they consent, grudgingly, to designing then they want to make useless objects, like ornaments and statuettes. I *love* designing plates and trays and tables and wastepaper baskets.'

His studios and showrooms are like a dream sequence in a film.

Eyes stare at you from white plates. Succulent fruit tempts you on a tray, but turns out to be painted. A table is laid with a cloth, silver and rolls of bread – all false. A ladder propped up against a wall is just a painted object on a screen.

For Fornasetti is the master of the *trompe-l'œil*, or art which tricks the eye, a style in which the Italians have been expert ever since the Renaissance.

He engraves every single design himself (and there are *hundreds* of them – Fornasetti is refreshingly prolific), and the design is printed on to china, wood, metal or composition, and then hand-painted.

Some of the designs are too elaborate, I think; many are exquisitely beautiful; none of them is dull. The whole collection if full of humour and excitement and variety.

And – happy tailpiece – you can find some of his things in a few of the best English shops.

14 October 1956

ALL MOD CONS WITH A ROBOT THROWN IN

Fasten your safety belt, lady, there's trouble ahead. Stop smiling indulgently when your husband talks of a ride on a rocket and your son runs around in a diver's helmet and calls himself the boy from Mars.

You've nothing to laugh at. Because the first bit of science fiction that's going to come true is strictly for women. *Look out within a decade for the electronic robot house.*

Plans for this dream house were mentioned a few days ago in a speech by Mr David Sarnoff, who is chairman of the giant Radio Corporation of America and has been for fifty years a pioneer of radio and electronics.

I cabled Mr Sarnoff and asked for a room-by-room description of the completely automatic home: and for his serious opinion of how soon the fiction would be fact.

There's a roving eye

'I see it in the near future,' he replied. 'The span between idea and execution is no longer measured in decades.'

Now let's go round the house.

'The **living room**', says Mr Sarnoff, 'will include a private colour TV set covering the whole house. By pressing switches you will be able to see what's going on everywhere. For instance, when a visitor rings the front door, a TV camera shows you who is there. You talk to the visitor and open the door without moving from the chair. In the same way you can watch the baby in the nursery. And you will be able to contact your husband at the office or while he's away on a fishing trip by a two-way radio worn on the wrist. **Your husband's study** will have a typewriter operated by speaking into it and an electronic accounting system which will swipe out the financial arrangements. It will compile the family's monthly bills and automatically instruct the bank to make payments. **The kitchen** will have all the obvious things like an infra-red cooker and electronic fridge, mixers and washing machine.

Everything under control

The really new thing will be a control panel which *stores* instructions. You will tell the control when to switch the oven on, do the washing, mix the dough, or take the meat from the refrigerator, and it will all be done at the right times. You can be miles away if you like.

The bedroom will have another TV screen for viewing the rest of the house. And it will have a sound absorber fitted into the bedhead above your pillow, so you can sleep undisturbed by traffic or planes.

The whole house will be heated or cooled by electronic panels, which operate silently and have no moving parts. There will be automatic eyes which close windows and doors as the weather changes. Lighting will be by panels, cleaning and dusting will be done by vibration. And the beginnings have been made in a home system for the instantaneous translation of languages.'

Well, thanks, Mr Sarnoff, for your help. I'm sure you mean well. I shall enjoy sitting, like Big Brother, at the controls of my master television set. My husband will just love it when I contact him on his fishing trips. Our bank manager will be delighted that our finances, if still unstable, are at least *clear.* It will be fun ringing up Finns and Yugoslavs and chatting freely with no language bars.

Just one small fear (or could it be hope?) lurks in the back of my mind.

THAT THE ELECTRONIC HOUSE MAY PROVE SO DARNED EXPENSIVE THAT WE SHAN'T BE ABLE TO AFFORD THE THING AT ALL.

BEST SMALL PLEASURE OF THE WEEK

By pure luck I dumped a handful of philadelphus in a jug and filled up with climbing 'Albertine' roses, to make the best flower arrangement I've ever done in my whole life. The apricot roses against the white, and the mingled scents, were delicious.

13 June 1957

ROSES, GOLD STARS, EVEN A TREE OF HEAVEN FOR MR WYATT

It's sixteen months since a celebrity dictated my column to me, and then it was Lady Pamela Berry.

This week the page comes courtesy of the bridegroom of the week, Mr Woodrow Wyatt, former MP and now the radiant star of *Panorama*.

I went with his beautiful bride, Lady Moorea, to see their new home in Regent's Park. But Mr Wyatt took charge.

'Let me help,' he said. 'I'll show you round and tell you what to say. You should describe me as a poverty-stricken ex-Labour MP. You can say that we have taken over a derelict house, but are painting it up as best we can. The back yard, as you see, it just a heap of rubble.

'By the way, what will you drink? I'm afraid there isn't anything much, but I could manage a cider cocktail.' I took it gratefully. It was a lovely strong one.

'Now we'll go round,' he said. 'First, you must see the one idea that was all my own.'

This is an interesting treatment of his study ceiling, which is papered with aquamarine wallpaper with huge gold stars.

'All the other ideas are my wife's,' he said, handsomely. 'Make a note of this one. There was a lot of ugly dark panelling on the walls, but we have papered it all white.'

Hypnotized like a TV interviewee, I wrote it down.

A bathroom idea

'Now here's another good touch. Speaking as a journalist, I think you should write about the bathroom. We hate clinical white bathrooms, so we've had it wallpapered with roses. You varnish the paper, of course, for a trifling extra cost.'

Next stop, the staircase. 'Stand here.' He placed me firmly in the right position. 'And look down. It is called the dancing staircase and the curves are rather fine.'

'Who was the architect?'

'Well, actually,' with a note of apology, 'it was Nash.'

At this point I fell down the top three stairs. 'Are you sure that it was a cider cocktail?' I asked. I was getting rather suspicious of this picture of the simple life.

Next stop. 'The dining room,' said Mr Wyatt. 'Make a note of the presents.'

This was sheer heaven. If there is one thing I enjoy, it's a good pick-over of wedding presents.

There were four toast racks from Richard Crossman.

A pink bathmat from Lady Cynthia Asquith, signed from 'Cynthia Quiz Asquith' (Remember she won £3000 on ITV?)

There was a silver dish from 'a jolly nice Trade Union man'. A Victorian history of the Palace of Westminster from John Betjeman. 'You could make a little joke about that,' suggested Mr Wyatt, 'as we are getting married in the Palace of Westminster.' (I've tried to think of a little joke, but it wouldn't come.) Some striped beach towels from John Braine of *Room at the Top*. Some smart silk table mats from the Philippine ambassador. And some Crown Derby knives from Lord Sieff.

We passed from the dining room to the 'small back yard', which is actually an enormous garden, and where, as with all true gardeners, Woodrow Wyatt's thoughts leapt into the future.

'I have been enquiring about quick-growing trees,' he said 'Quite soon the garden will be shaded with silver birches and Tree of Heaven.'

On this peaceful note I closed my notebook, and thanked him gratefully for his help.

'What are you going to wear for the wedding?' I asked Lady Moorea.

'A silver-blue dress and a hat to match. Woodrow helped me choose them.'

'Oh, yes,' he said, 'I gave my views.'

That's the joy of marrying a politician. No vagueness, dithering or indifference.

They have views on *everything*.

NOTES

Woodrow Wyatt, Baron Wyatt of Weeford (1918–1997) Politician, journalist and broadcaster.

Lady Moorea Hastings (1928–2011) Married to Woodrow Wyatt 1957–1966, later married to Brinsley Black.

Richard 'Dick' Crossman (1907–1974) Labour Party MP.

Lady Cynthia Asquith (1887–1960) English writer and socialite.

Lord Sieff (1913–2001) Marcus, youngest son of Israel and Rebecca Marks. On the board of Marks and Spencer from 1954. He became joint managing director of the company in 1967 and chairman in 1972.

---

29 July 1957

THE UNDERGROUND IS WORKING FOR ME

Two weeks ago we moved house. And while I perched like a stork on top of a ladder, holding up the ceiling with one hand and steadying the ladder with the other, with a hammer sticking out of my belt and some 2-inch tacks between my teeth, I discovered how to beat inflation.

'You'll never fix a pelmet board *that* way,' said the man from the Big Firm who was laying the carpet. 'Better let me come round one evening and put it up properly.'

Since then I have lived in the centre of a network of Little Men. I have discovered that the entire British nation is working by itself and *for* itself in its spare time.

People who say the British don't work hard are talking nonsense. But half the work is going underground.

If Mr Thorneycroft could get our unofficial production figures he would find they are simply enormous. They would make the Germans and the Japanese look silly.

I have drunk gallons of tea in the kitchen with men who are working by day for big contractors and shops and works and councils, and are doubling up for private people at evenings and weekends.

They go for the spare-time work because (a) they don't pay tax on it and (b) 'there's none of the muckin' about.'

The first joy speaks for itself. There is nothing like a lump of good cold cash in the pocket.

The second counts almost as highly. I have heard the phrase 'muckin' about' from twenty different people.

'If you could see me working for the council, you'd be disgusted,' said my electrician. 'You'd never employ me. Takes me days sometimes to join a couple of wires. Nobody's fault really, but just muckin' about waitin' for things to arrive.'

'Tomorrow I'll only be muckin' about on the new estate,' said my painter. 'So I'll be here fresh as a daisy at 7 p.m.'

'I like this sort of work,' said my carpenter.' I can plan the whole job myself from start to finish. Now, at the works, there's one man puts the screws in, and another man puts the nails in, and half the time you don't even know what you're making. Could be a sentry box. Could be a dog kennel. For a skilled man, it's just muckin' about.'

This spare-time Underground Movement is large and well organized.

The spare-time carpenter has a pal who is a spare-time electrician, whose brother-in-law is a spare-time plumber, whose step-father is a spare-time plasterer.

All their wives are spare-time dressmakers and their mothers and sisters are spare-time upholstresses.

I don't know what the morals are of employing the Underground. I started off myself through the proper channels.

But when I found that the electricity people wouldn't look at me for days, that the builders wouldn't touch me for weeks, and nobody wanted to make me a cupboard *ever*, I sank gratefully on to the bosom of the *maquis*.

So I'm sure it's a waste of good breath to talk of working harder to boost production. Most of the little men are *pale* with overwork.

The thing is to get all this energy crackling above board – instead of below.

Anne photobombing Princess
Margaret and Lord Snowdon.

Anne and Food

I certainly wasn't brought up to believe that food is just for sustenance. Anne loved eating – rather fast if the truth were known. As a family we tend to suck food down rather than extensively chewing every mouthful. We are also very bad at waiting. Obviously when posh dining is involved we can behave, but at a family encounter it is each man or woman for themselves. Anne could certainly be on 'seconds' before the carver had got round the table. She preferred to be carved for (served first, on account of seniority). She was also quite dictatorial about how the various joints should be carved: 'It's a shoulder you know. Cut it across – NO, smaller slices.' The instruction being quite unnecessary as we usually had a shoulder of lamb, but it served as part of the Sunday ritual.

When I was a small child Nanny cooked for me. I was taught how to balance peas on the back of my fork, a talent that I don't think I still retain. Fish fingers first made an appearance in 1955, and Nanny was hot on to the trend. I had to protest when they appeared too often. Sugar only came off the ration in September 1953, when I was two, and the Scott-James household quickly made up for its absence. Cakes, jellies, sweets, fizzy drinks – my teeth never recovered. When plain yogurt first appeared in a commercial tub, there was a ceremonial opening, Anne cheering it up no end with the inclusion of lashings of double cream and many spoonfuls of demerara. I thought it ambrosia. Fuller's Walnut Cake was often served at tea. It is impossible to describe the deliciousness of the white sugary frosting that coated the double layer of walnut sponge sandwiched together with buttercream. It came in a white box with a clear film window. A proper sort of cake.

We didn't do snacking. The odd packet of Smiths' Crisps, maybe with a fizzy drink before lunch on a Sunday, but nothing serious. Anne was thin, and believed the 'moment on the lips' theory. She wrote extensive pieces on diet, and was not afraid to mention it if she thought I had put on weight. I was, of course, thanks to genetics, very skinny in youth. The mother of my best friend once enquired if my mother was worried? No. Neither was I. We ate the most exquisite food.

Food took a gastro leap at the end of the fifties with the arrival of a cook – Martha Todd. A slim, formal individual who appeared every day to cater for the greedies. Martha was fastidiously tidy and always attired in a short-sleeved white overall. Her kitchen was kept immaculate. We never had fridges and cupboards full of food. Martha cooked on and for the day. She really came into her own when Anne married Osbert, and she was able to excel. In the tiny box kitchen in Eaton Square she produced the most extraordinary menus, bussed down to the dining room in a dumb waiter. Roulades and mousses, little fish dishes in cheese sauce, savoury and sweet soufflés, and Martha's *pièce de résistance*, a tower of profiteroles, light puffs of delight dripping in a rich chocolate sauce. Meringues were a constant, made by Martha in her spare moments and kept in a tin, as were the crumbly almond crescent biscuits that she made for tea. God, they were good. Looking back it is odd how little I knew about her private life. Martha was a doer not a chatterer. She was married to a Mr Todd (never seen) and was German, but that is my entire sum of knowledge. As a child my interest did not extend past the front door, and as soon as she left the flat I gave her life little thought. Of course, I wish I had.

There was a rumour, *possibly* apocryphal, that Princess Margaret had attempted to poach Martha away, after attending a dinner at our house. I remember the dinner. Well, you sort of would. Tony decided at the last minute to invite his friend Derek Hart for the evening. It was a formal dinner following a first night at Covent Garden. Anne was furious and decided there was no room around the table, so a lonely tray was assembled in the drawing room for the unwanted guest. I remember saying to Mother that it was going to make for an odd evening, one guest languishing in Coventry. In the end Derek was a no-show. Anyway, Margaret ended the evening having a row with Tony. Tony left. Five minutes later Margaret swept out too. Everyone stood dumbstruck, appalled at the idea of PM alone on the streets looking for a cab. There was a huge kerfuffle and a male guest rushed out to act as escort and security. All in all a thrilling evening. Anyway, there was no question of Anne losing Martha. PM didn't come again and Martha stayed by our stove souffléing away.

Anne loved restaurants. We often visited The Seven Stars (part of the Lyons corner house group) when I was young, and my brother home from school. Roasts concealed under silver salvers were wheeled round the tables on trollies, and it all seemed rather grand. Wheeler's was a favourite of my father's and we also made the odd foray to the River Room at the Savoy, but Anne really did prefer pubs and Italian trattorias.

One of the few areas where Osbert and Mother parted ways was eating out. Osbert did not like restaurants (unless they were beside a Grecian sea), but loved eating at the Garrick Club. He could not see why it was not a treat for Anne, who was allowed in for 'ladies' night'. Of course she admired the look of the club, but the food back in the day was not the best or the most imaginative. We would tease Osbert mercilessly at the appearance of the requisite half-avocado, and the mashed potato served by the scoop.

The Italians were just taking over the London restaurant scene in the 1960s and how much jollier they were From the breezy chat of the waiters, to the sticky spare ribs served at our local favourite, Mimmo d'Ischia, not to mention the tables squished up (a particular bugbear to O) so tightly you could listen with ease to the chat not only of the table next door, but also the one next door to that. This was a necessity, as the acoustics were such you certainly couldn't hear much across your own – no hardship, as the banter was usually of quite a high standard and provided much amusement when we got home.

Mother never minded eating out alone. She didn't take a book or a newspaper to pass the time, just herself. Perfectly happy just observing the clientele. Neither was she averse to taking a restaurant to task if she wasn't happy. I cherish a conversation with a hapless manager over the provenance of a Dover sole. I wanted to warn him that seated at his table was a woman more than familiar with the product. 'This is a lemon sole,' said Anne, looking with disdain at the hapless fish as it was placed with a flourish in front of her, 'I asked for Dover.' 'This *is* a Dover sole, Madam. Bought in the market this morning,' came the confident reply. 'No, it is not. This sole is false. A false sole. I have eaten sole my entire life. This is a lemon sole.' 'I can assure you, Madam . . .' He had a last vain try, before the sad imposter was removed in disgrace, and glasses of chilled Chablis arrived to placate his client. As long as you were not on the receiving end, the quick demolition of the opposition, could be quite stimulating. Not long after, the restaurant closed down. A sole too far . . .

Anne did cook at the weekends, and the food was always very good. Roast on a Sunday, apple charlotte, Irish stews and shepherd's pie. Excellent English fare. But I do also recall a period in the mid-sixties when Vesta Beef Curry hit the menu in a big way – usually for a Friday supper or a Saturday lunch. I thought it very sophisticated. Boil-in- the-bag rice accompanied by a packet of strange brown, dried cubes that swelled when you mixed in water. Anne added her own touches – sliced fresh banana, and papadums that she fried in oil in the kitchen leaving clouds of black smoke in her wake. Mango chutney was also part of the side selection. We all thought it a delicious treat. Really we could have been in Bombay. Apparently you can still buy it. I am rather tempted, but loath to risk disappointment.

Anne didn't keep a well stocked fridge, no real need in town with Martha on tap. Later in her life, there was always just enough to cobble together a delicious snack. I could absolutely guarantee to find the fridge entirely bare, bar one shelf which would contain:

a packet of smoked salmon
a small loaf of Hovis
a small container of cream
a small pre-washed packet of watercress
a box of six eggs
a half-bottle of champagne (for me, Anne didn't really like it)

That would be it. The necessities for life.

Anne also had a 'signature dish', which was absolutely delicious. Fillets of John Dory cooked in the pan and finished off with cream and Noilly Prat. I would make it now, but Noilly Prat is not one of my cupboard staples.

20 November 1955

WAITER . . . BRING ON THE ROAST PORK.

'Take 12 pairs of frogs' legs . . .' Bah!
'Take one œuf sur le plat . . .' Bah!

Soon, someone has got to talk sense about food, so it had better be me. I'm out to kill the garlic cult, the fried rice fetish, the paprika complex. I'm tipping you to look out for a great resurgence of English cooking.

You can keep all the recipes which begin 'Wash and dry 12 pairs of frogs' legs' or 'Pound some garlic in a mortar' (*give me a slice of roast pork with a hunk of crackling*).

You can keep all the cookbooks which plop on my desk every week with recipes from Mexico, Saudi-Arabia, Mitteleuropa, and Central France (*give me an apple tart with a dollop of Devonshire cream*).

You can keep your kous-kous and aubergines and smorgasbord and that blanched sickly Continental meat called veal (*give me a jacket potato and a buttony Brussels sprout*).

As a matter, not of opinion but of sheer hard fact, our meat is again the best in the world, our cheese-making, which nearly died, is better than ever, our fish is unequalled, from the oyster to the kipper, and no foreign apples can live with a Cox's Orange Pippin.

I went to dinner this week in a small London hotel where the menu was based on English Country House cooking.

- **Hare soup**
- **Grilled sole on the bone**
- **Roast saddle of mutton with creamed artichokes, Brussels sprouts with chestnuts, jacket potatoes and redcurrant jelly**
- **Jumbles**
- **Five sorts of biscuits, including Bath Olivers and hot Scotch oatcakes, with three sorts of cheese**
- **And Cox's Orange Pippins and Kentish cobs**

Oh my, what a meal.

Don't imagine I ate all of it. I conked out at the cheese.

It reminded me of what Coleridge said: '**a man who refuses apple dumplings cannot have a pure mind**.'

17 February 1957

A MEMO FROM PARIS

A memo from Paris to Paddington, Liverpool Street, Charing Cross, New Street Station, Birmingham, Edinburgh Waverley and Manchester Central.

One of the crackerjack restaurants of France – two stars and four spoons and forks in Michelin – is situated in a Paris station: the Relais of the Gare de l'Est.

Travellers on night trains arrive early and get their strength up on *Tournedos Curnonsky or Coquilles St Jacques à la façon des gastronomes*. They get their strength up still further on wine chosen from a cellar of 30,000,000 bottles.

Dozens of Parisians come to lunch or dine here who are not catching any trains at all. (*Imagine bowling off to celebrate your birthday at St Pancras*.)

Banquets and dinner parties are held in the banqueting room next to the restaurant. (*Imagine inviting two hundred guests to a dinner in Cannon-Street*.)

The restaurant is not run by the French railways, but is wisely left by them to M. Gabriel Lavrut, a well-known gastronome.

Right lines

Sixteen other railway restaurants in France are run on gourmet lines and the number is growing.

British Railways – take the Brown Windsor soup off the menus. Bring on the *Soupe à l'oignon gratinée*.

Take off the baked cod and boiled potatoes. Bring on the *Sole farcie à la mode du chef*.

Anne posing for *Picture Post*.

9 June 1957

WE REALLY HAD GRAVY SOUP . . .

I am not going to let any catering organizations, British travel associations, or come-to-Britain clubs soft-soap me. Our hotel catering is *not* getting any better. We stopped last Saturday at an hotel which had an excellent write-up in Raymond Postgate's 1957 *Good Food Guide*. The meal we got reads like a tired old American joke about British cooking.

We *really* had: gravy soup, *turbot maître d'hotel* (fish in a gluey white sauce), shreds of meat with potatoes, tinned peas and tinned carrots, and a choice of prunes and semolina or ice cream.

The menu said cabbage and broad beans, but they were 'off' by 1.15. Semolina is a substance I didn't know existed for anyone out of a baby chair.

I am not attacking the *Good Food Guide*, which is an honest attempt to do an English Michelin, and is edited without strings or bias. The few good places I do know are all in it.

Hotels and restaurants, *when* will you chuck your pretentious menus and your French-names dishes and your five-course lunches with everything decent 'off'? And serve two or three honest, well-cooked dishes. It will be easier and cheaper for you, and more exciting for us.

15 September 1957

JUST CUT
THE CACKLE

I am not well up in egg politics, but I do know this much: if the egg farmers, egg packers, and egg retailers don't stop talking about eggs, we shall soon be a non-egg-eating nation.

I am a keen egg lover, and the best egg scrambler in five continents (the secret being to take the pan off the flame before the eggs are set). But I am beginning to get very queasy about eggs, suspecting them all of being past their prime.

I now crack them at arm's length, fearing a cloud of hydrogen sulphide. I stop at country cottages and try to buy them direct from the hen.

I test shop eggs by dropping them in a pan of water to see if they sink or swim. I never thought of this before.

My advice to the egg tycoons is: cut the Lion and cut the cackle.

The way to enjoy an egg is not to think about it.

NOTE
The Lion mark was originally launched in the 1950s to indicate which eggs were British.

Top row: Clare, John Piper and Osbert. Bottom row: Diana Murray, John Betjeman and Myfanwy Piper. (I am not reading, by the way, just keeping score.)

Anne and Leisure

R eading, reading and then some more reading. With a pile of books by her side, Anne was perfectly happy.

She did enjoy listening to music at home, but it was never for background noise. Anne liked to concentrate entirely on one activity or the other. If the gramophone or radio were playing, she would sit and give the music her full attention. If she wanted to read, then she did so in silence. And reading always took priority.

Any television that came into the house lived in the spare room, and I became the addict, not Anne. The only programmes I ever recall her watching with regularity were, rather predictably, *The Forsyte Saga*, *Upstairs, Downstairs* and *Civilisation*; but weeks would go by without her tuning in the set. She might check out a sitcom, and she enjoyed *That Was The Week That Was*, but this was partly for work. Anne did not like to think anything had passed her by, and this included the latest popular culture.

She was also surprisingly interested in sport. Wimbledon was her big treat of the year (she had played a lot of tennis in her youth), and each year the Scott-James page committed to covering the women's game – anything from Gorgeous Gussie's pants to the lack of showmanship displayed by many women on court. Anne said they risked becoming 'dull, dull, dull', citing Christine Truman as an example. Osbert bought the first Sony Trinitron so Anne could watch the grass and players in glorious colour. I still have it – and, thrillingly, it works.

Mother also enjoyed watching cricket and rugby, knowing the names of all the players and, more impressively, the rules, which I never got to grips with. I think she had a rugby-playing boyfriend at university, so had spent time on the touchline.

Television may have failed to spark her imagination, but the cinema definitely succeeded. Anne loved it. Usually going alone, and happy to watch almost any genre of film. Obviously she had been brought up with the Hollywood musicals and loved Fred Astaire, although her film star of choice was James Stewart. She didn't usually bother to see musicals in the theatre, although she made an exception for *My Fair Lady* and *West Side Story* to the extent that we had the LPs and she played them quite regularly, humming along to the tunes. Anne was a keen hummer, although a tuneless one. You would often hear her humming around the garden, or in the kitchen. The sound usually did not relate to any song or piece of music, and was always a sign of happiness rather than anxiety.

Anne asked for the song 'I Feel Pretty' from *West Side Story* for one of her choices on *Desert Island Discs*. And it is a very 'Anne' song – Maria is transported by love and happiness, unaware that her lover lies dying from stab wounds at the rumble. 'We weren't put on this earth to have fun.'

I took her to see a fabulous and very louche production of *Cabaret* with Alan Cumming starring as the M.C. My daughter, Calypso, then about ten, came along with us. The style of the production meant we all sat at small club tables with the actors lasciviously gyrating in close proximity. Mother must have spent half the performance studying Calypso, who was wide-eyed with interest. I think it was during a rendition of 'Bee-dle-dee . . . Two ladies' that Anne leant across our table to mutter *sotto voce*, 'Do you think this is *entirely* suitable, dear?' (Probably not, but hey-ho.)

Her parents were keen theatregoers, and from a young age the family were taken regularly to queue up for the cheap seats in the pit; and these early forays established her enthusiasm for the stage. They were a far cry from her visits to Glyndebourne and Covent Garden with Osbert, when it was usually a first night and distinctly glam. If they visited Glyndebourne, they had dinner first with Moran Caplat, an old friend and the beating heart of the opera company. Both Anne and Osbert had close ties to Glyndebourne, Osbert for his stage designs and costumes, Anne for a book she wrote in conjunction with Christopher Lloyd on the gardens.

When I was a child, nothing gave Anne greater satisfaction than a little DIY, and she could often be found engaged in a bit of craft. In London she had a moment when no wardrobe was safe. The door panels contrast-papered with blowsy flower patterns from wallpaper leftovers.

Anne was much taken with Copydex when it first appeared in the sixties. The white rubber glue had an odd fishy odour but this did not put Mother off; she got through tubes of it. Trim was a source of delight. Cotton pompom fringe was bought by the yard from Peter Jones and glued round lampshades and tin wastepaper baskets. Annoyingly, after a while the braid turned brown – something in the mix. She was also a fan of patchwork, and would spend hours cutting the card templates, to make tablecloths, bedspreads, and borders for the cottage curtains. Osbert's first wife had been an expert embroiderer, so Anne rather eschewed this pastime, until I appeared one day with a

Reading with Mother.
From left to right : Marie, Anne, Violet and John.

tapestry kit, after which her competitive streak took over and she went out and bought an identical pack, and would spend hours working away at it, comparing our stitching techniques.

Mother was not a fan of board games, or cards. We had all the games, but it was my father who taught me chess, mahjong (although don't ask me to build a wall now), patience and l'attaque. Anne did enjoy a spirited round of racing demon, and also took to trivial pursuit, although useless on any science subject. She would have been an excellent 'phone a friend', as long as you kept her on topic.

For Mother, leisure and work crossed over. Everything fed in some way or another back into her writing, and even when she was relaxing her notebook was by her side. 'My working life consists of moving around and talking to people and writing. When I get a holiday, like a piece of wound-up clockwork, I move around and talk to people and write.'

Holidays, food, the arts, gardening, home life, politics, even friends – all provided the weekly oxygen for her page.

And, always, it was words that she turned to when she needed to switch off.

If reading books was central, writing was even more so. Through the self-expression of writing she found a release.

THE U CULT THAT WILL DRIVE YOU CRAZY

Two days ago I caught a crowded, stuffy plane to Paris and drove quickly to the best hotel. There I fortified myself with a U lunch, changed into a U suit, rubbed up my shoes with a duster, pulled on clean U gloves, got in a U car, and – worrying like mad about my vowel sounds, terrified lest I forget myself and say 'Pardon', 'Pleased to meet you' or 'Bye-bye ' – I drove to pay a U call on Miss Nancy Mitford.

Why was I in such a social dither ?

Because Miss Mitford is the international arbiter of taste and fashion. She wrote a famous essay last year on U (or upper class) manners, and has now followed up with a book on the subject.

Called *Noblesse Oblige*, it comes out next week.

The book is an 'Enquiry into the Identifiable Characteristics of the English Aristocracy'. It is extremely funny, it's sure to sell tens of thousands – and it's authoritative.

For Miss Mitford herself, chic, handsome, brilliant, is impeccably aristocratic; and most of the contributors are either members of the upper classes or good working imitations.

Most of *Noblesse Oblige* is devoted to upper-class *language*. (Though it does toss out a few useful general maxims, such as 'When drunk, gentlemen often become amorous or maudlin or vomit in public, but they never become truculent.')

So I thought I would ask Miss Mitford to extend the range and give me a few classic examples of U and non-U fashions and behaviour.

This took a bit of time. Miss Mitford said it was a question that needed notice. But at last she proclaimed three non-U brand marks.

1. Women in trousers
2. Men who comb their hair in public
3. Anything in plastic

'Now, what happens if you are not born U?' I asked. 'Can you become U?'

'Yes, I think so, if you go to Eton.'

'But if you are too old for Eton? Or if you are a girl?'

'Then your chance is small.'

'Would you say', I said, 'that people of great personality can transcend these customs?'

'Oh yes, of course. For instance the late Lord Beauchamp would only drink champagne out of a jug.'

'Don't you think', I asked, 'that U usage changes? For instance, we were brought up on *scent* and *stays*. But the forces of publicity have pressed *perfume and corsets* so hard that perhaps these vulgar words could now be accepted?'

'Absolutely not,' said Miss Mitford. 'They make me shudder.'

'Is my behaviour U?' I said.

'You have U legs,' she said, kindly.

I felt more relaxed. 'How seriously do you take U standards?' I asked. She laughed and her huge intelligent grey eyes sparkled.

'Of course, not seriously at all. It's a ridiculous joke which started by accident. I wrote an essay for a magazine and it was two pages short. So I filled up with a few comments on upper-class language. They started a snowball which grew so large that I have had to produce a book about it. I know I shall be violently attacked for my snobbery – I always am. But of course it is written with irony, it's not a Book of Etiquette.'

As I looked round the lovely room, with its Sheraton desk and porcelain lamps, out to the romantic little garden, all ivy and trees, and then back to Miss Mitford herself, very Parisian in a white wool blouse and black skirt, I thought that if she ever wrote a *serious* book on manners, I'd even read that too.

Of course, the best thing about this U book is that every line is inflame with controversy.

Greens (it says) is non-U for U vegetables.
This is not always true. A gardener uses greens as a specialist word. He means Brussels tops and spinach, as opposed to onions or peas.

The upper class (it says) has an aversion to high tea.
But what about ham and egg tea after a day with the Pytchley or the Quorn?

There is a statement about a gentleman never getting truculent when drunk.
But one scion of a very famous family gets fighting drunk three times a week.

Altogether, Miss Mitford has stirred up a splendid potful of laughter and wrath.
We are all going to laugh about U and non-U manners for weeks to come.

OH, HOW I LOATHE WEEKENDS!

I know it's like kicking a dog or slinging mud at the flag, but I am ratting on one of our most famous and finest customs: the British weekend.

Foreign visitors are always astonished at the general post which takes place here from Friday to Monday. Townees rush to the country, country people rush to the town, and everyone rushes to the sea. All in name of rest and a healthy change.

I have had just about enough of those dreadful little refreshers. For sheer relaxation, give me any office, factory, shipyard or salt mine.

Whether you're going to your own country hideout, planting yourself on friends, taking the enormous risk of an hotel, or taking your turn to play hostess to the other migrants, the weekend is becoming more and more of a Commando course.

Going to your own hideout?
The journey alone is worse than your working week. Either you start at a convenient time and drive for two or three hours in a mad charge of cars like a stock car race. Or you avoid the rush, leave late on a Friday night, and arrive for your weekend rest around two in the morning. Or you play it really safe and leave Thursday, but if you do this often enough, you will be out of a job.

But there are worse hazards on the journey than traffic. You may have been mad enough to take the children.

On our usual route west there is a dismal lorry-drivers' pull-up at an unbelievably unattractive spot near Slough. This sad café is beloved by my children because it serves corned beef sandwiches and has a favourite mangy marmalade cat.

Two hundred yards short of the place to an inch, my daughter turns ashy pale and is sick, and only a corned beef sandwich can bring her round.

In the last few miles you may experience a lift in the spirit. You admire the swelling sticky buds, and the hedgerows in the new green veils.

But what a shock when you see the garden You left it so prim and tidy last Sunday night. In five days the jungle has taken over. The clipped lawns have become hayfields, and the seedlings strangled by bindweed. Two days relentless work will scarcely put it right.

Planting yourself on friends? You must have forgotten the frightful discomfort of other people's houses.

The ghastly cold of the manor house where the system which is laughingly called central heating is always switched off on 1 April.

The bohemian habits of your friends with the cosy cottage where 'we all just eat and sleep and do as we please.'

They never told you your room would be the ex-nursery and your bed a four-foot cot. Or that they streamline breakfast and lunch so that your first bite of the day (delayed by endless drinks at the local) will be at 2 o'clock in the afternoon.

OR – playing the gracious hostess The strains and stresses of this sort of weekend cannot be listed in a fourteen-page paper, but I will isolate three.

Crating the garden produce for guests to take home.

Enduring other people's children (makes you regard your own with quite a friendly eye).

The cost of the drinks.

Yes, I envy the independent characters who keep their weekends free, have time to shop, to see friends, and get to the hairdresser and see all the new plays.

While I spend the best years of my life on the Great West Road.

GO JUMP OFF THE PIER!

Thank goodness the Island Race is getting soft. More and more people are saying quite openly that they cannot stand up to the rigours of the English seaside.

When I was young, it was a matter of pride to sneak into the water when the red flag was flying above the boiling grey sea.

Not for the world would we have missed our daily blow on the pier – there was always a sporting chance that one of us would blow over in a squall.

And *how* we enjoyed the morning race for a choice spot under the breakwater, where, fortified by biscuits and hot cocoa, we would sit in macintoshes inhaling the supposedly healthy smell of decaying seaweed, until we had to tear ourselves away for lunch.

Since the war, I have been bored to death during two wet weeks in Swanage. Card games, ping-pong and teashops by day and the whole town asleep by 10 at night.

I have shivered in Jersey with sea so rough that the fishermen couldn't get out to their lobster pots.

Every day some new disappointment for the children – no bathing or a cancelled picnic.

And I have twiddled my thumbs in Frinton, which is so refined there isn't a cinema.

Well, I'm not going to do it any more. It's all too disappointing and too dull.

I'm not going to bathe in an icy sea, picnic on a windswept beach or die of boredom in the evenings. My future plans are clear.

I shall pack up the children and take them south. It's high time they learnt about garlic and siestas and heard the buzzing of the cicadas and the drum-roll of bullfrogs in a marsh.

No, the English seaside holiday is a fine thing for building the character.

But, like cold baths and smacking, it's on the way out.

3 March 1957

IN ANGER

In rapid follow-on to a sugary book by Mrs Clare Luce's secretary comes *Working for the Windsors* by *their* secretary Dina Wells Hood.

As all decent secretaries are loyal to their employers, these books are usually emasculated and pointless.

What I am looking for is a ruthless exposé of some famous woman by an embittered secretary fired in anger.

'Took down thirteen letters that day, mostly illiterate. I put them into some sort of English as I went along.'

'It was her custom to arrive in the office about noon, read her personal letters, and leave shortly for lunch with you-know-who. The afternoon would be a write-off.'

'Her greatest ability was for getting things free.'

'Sometimes she brought her children to the office, and would leave them in the reception room all day. It was my task to give them lunch, take them to a film, and later send them home in a cab if she forgot them.'

This would be much more readable. I suggest that secretaries who are bound by loyalties should leave biography to the uninhibited outsider.

NOTE
Clare Boothe Luce (1903–1987) Author, politician and the first American woman to hold a major ambassadorial post (appointed Ambassador to Italy in 1952). Married to Henry Luce, the founder of the *Time* empire.

---

25 May 1957

FIGHTS, JEALOUSY – BUT THEY STILL LOVED . . .

I have just read an extraordinary book about a happy marriage. A marriage littered with violent rows, wrecked by drink, and hideous with Hogarthian squalor.

But a marriage far happier than that of millions of well-preserved couples whose relationship is polite, friendly and utterly arid. **Because Dylan and Caitlin Thomas were passionately interested in each other until the day Dylan Thomas died.**

Leftover Life to Kill is by Dylan Thomas's widow, and I don't believe a woman has ever let her hair down so completely in print before. She hasn't got an inhibition. *She sees her husband with the piercing eye of a caricaturist.*

'A broken-comb-toothed mouth, dark glasses and clothes which, it was evident, had never been put on, and off; but had taken root, in the barren soil, and were growing on him.'

She sees his character as sharply as his physique

'His passion for lies was congenital: more a practice in invention than a lie. He would tell quite unnecessary ones, which did not in any way improve his situation; such as when he had been to one cinema, saying it was another.'

She recalls every blow of their frequent battles

'The house rattled, and banged and thudded, and groaned with our murder of each other. But these fights, which were an essential part of our everyday life, and became fiercer and more deadly at each onslaught, so that you could have sworn no two people reviled each other more; and could never, under any fabulous change of circumstances, come together again: were almost worthwhile because, when the reconciliation did take place, according to how long we could stick it out, it was so doubly, trebly, quadruply sweet.'

She writes without flinching of his infidelity

'These thieves of my love, which I was so presumptuously sure was mine only, I bitterly and jealously resented, with all the primitive catfish instincts that I didn't even know were there, and the vile, sinking, retching lurch, that jealousy engenders.'

But I still say it was a happy marriage. In spite of the fighting and the tempests the Thomases loved each other passionately, and her life was a desert when he died.

Her book is not an exposé or a shocker.

It is the story of a marriage on a grand scale, brilliantly written and violently felt.

Read it.

7 July 1957

LIFE WITH A GENIUS

First Caitlin Thomas's stormy book about life with Dylan Thomas. Now Maurice Goudeket's gentle book called *Close to Colette*.

Two utterly opposite pictures of married life with a genius.

I have been talking to M. Goudeket, who was happily married for thirty years to the wise and wonderful Colette, author of *Chéri* and *Gigi* and some fifty other books, who was not only a world celebrity when he met her, while he was an obscure businessman, but who was seventeen years older than he.

It seems to have been a marriage of complete devotion. They did not have to master any problems, because the obvious problems did not exist.

'I never felt I was married to a celebrity,' M. Goudeket told me, 'because Colette took up no attitude herself. She was completely practical and of this world, and was unaware of being an extraordinary person. She was not a conscious "character" like Hemingway . . . who has to live up to being Hemingway. She never felt she was Colette. Remember she was a French provincial through and through, with an intense closeness to everyday things.' (In the book he describes how 'she knew a recipe for everything, whether it was for furniture polish, vinegar, orange wine or quince water, for cooking truffles or preserving linen and materials. Pickling and steeping held no mystery for her, and everything smelt good and healthy.')

'Then I, for my part,' said M. Goudeket, 'never thought of her as a celebrity, but only as a wife. I never took a note of anything she said. If there was a problem, it was in the early years, when I had to overcome a hostility which her friends and the public felt towards me – because in marrying her I had taken something away from *them*. Mel Ferrer had the same problem when he married Audrey Hepburn, although he is a charming fellow. In time I think, people got used to me as Colette's husband. Some of her friends', he said to me, sweetly, 'even got to like me.'

The book is not a connected story of Colette's life. It is rambling and anecdotal, but full of charm.

Colette turning up for the maiden voyage of the *Normandie* with her basket of provisions . . . homemade pâté, cold chicken and hard-boiled eggs.

Colette at Saint-Tropez, taking her cat for a walk in the vineyard every morning, then gardening with the cat and dog always by her side.

Here are the sunlight and the artichokes and the slatted shutters and the loaves and wine that are the joy and essence of provincial France.

15 September 1957

THE WESTERN GOES BOOM

It's a strange experience, as you stand chopping up onions for dinner, to hear a pistol shot and the thunder of galloping hooves.

It means, of course that someone has switched on the TV to watch one of the thirteen Westerns which will be running this autumn.

Westerns are booming fantastically. It has just been announced that in America thirty-three cowboy films will run every week from October. I am told you can hardly find room to sit down in Texas, Colorado or Arizona for the film units and camera crews. Here *Gun Law* is the connoisseur's choice, but you take your pick from a fine list which includes *Rin Tin Tin*, *The Sheriff of Cochise*, *Brave Eagle*, *Hopalong Cassidy*, *The Lone Ranger*, *Wells Fargo*, *Champion the Wonder Horse*, and the *Zane Grey Theatre*.

Make no mistake about these being only for children. Many are shown in the evenings, and men of intellect and distinction hurry home for *Wells Fargo* at 7 o'clock and refuse to dine out on Mondays. In country houses wives complain that they have to do all the entertaining while their husbands stare at the set.

Eric Ambler loves watching Westerns, though '*Gun Law* is the only one I will drop something else to see. I think that some of the episodes have the Maupassant touch, and the level of insight into the characters is quite high. The others are boringly moral with ideas of nursery simplicity. I suppose I watch them as a kind of irritant.'

John Braine of *Room at the Top* tells me he would like to write a Western. 'I'd like to live in America for a year and get the real clean atmosphere of the old West. I hate prettified Westerns.

'I like them very violent, with lots of bodies and the true smell of cordite.'

Frankie More O'Ferrall can't be torn from *The Lone Ranger*, nor Sir Alliott Verdon-Roe, the great aircraft designer, from *Champion the Wonder Horse*.

Don't ask me for any deep significance in all this. It's not my line.

But it's a big year for the bronco, the sheriff, the hoister and the saloon.

NOTES

Eric Ambler (1909–1998) Thriller writer, considered by many to have invented the modern suspense novel.

John Braine (1922–1987) Writer whose first novel, *Room at the Top* (1957), defined the 'angry young man' of the 1950s.

Frankie More O'Ferrall (1904–1976) Founder of the Anglo-Irish Bloodstock Agency.

Sir Alliottt Verdon-Roe (1877–1958) Aircraft designer and manufacturer – and the first Englishman to construct and fly his own aeroplane.

WHAT FUN! SEE HOW OUR IDOLS ARE TOPPLING

What a nation we are for loathing success. We're such good losers that we can't endure a winner. A few idols have toppled this week, and their fall has been greeted with wolfish glee.

FRANÇOISE SAGAN has brought out a bad third novel. What joy. What bliss. 'Françoise flops', 'Adieu, success', 'Françoise exploded', write the happy critics. 'One more book like this', says another, hopefully, 'and she'll be back in oblivion.'

A flop – we're glad

The fact is Françoise is a brilliant girl who deservedly made a packet. This excites the French, delights the Americans, who worship success, especially in the young. It's all part of their vitality.

But it disgusts the sourpuss English. We don't say, ' Alas, she's flopped' but 'She's flopped, hooray.'

Why so happy?

But why be so *happy* when last year's genius has a play turned down and writes a dreary book? We ought to be awfully sad.

All the autumn we've been letting off fireworks to celebrate the fiascos of successful people.

VIVIEN LEIGH Good, *she* made an ass of herself, first in the House of Lords and then over her holiday.

CHARLIE CHAPLIN Good, we've been waiting like vultures for him for years.

The person we've taken to our hearts this week is **JUDY GARLAND**, because she's had such terrible failures. Illnesses, rows, breakdowns, and a long bad patch as a star; all this makes her fit for us to love.

And for my own bête noire **GRACE KELLY**, whom I dislike for no reason at all, except that she's so perfect – I shall throw my hat into the air when she comes a cropper.

To the British success is *indecent* unless you're old, ugly or unhappy. Then – good losers that we are – we rally round.

Osbert's drawing of Maudie Littlehampton chatting
to Anne. George Weidenfeld and Bernard Levin loiter
in the background.

Anne and Parties

Parties are by their very nature random, raucous affairs, and this did not fit well with Anne's personality. There was nothing about Anne that was random or raucous. Neither are parties suitable events for the short or the tall, as a crowded room makes it virtually impossible to understand a word anyone is saying to you. Those of normal size can relish sparkling repartee and flirtatious encounters, but for Anne it meant looking down on to moving lips and meaningless smiles, in a pretence to engage.

Anne did go to dances while she was at Oxford, but in later life should she mention dancing it was usually to say that she doubted whether she and Osbert would ever have become a couple had they met in youth, as due to their disparate heights they would have appeared idiotic on the dance floor.

Anne saved her particular ire for the cocktail party, where food was virtually non-existent and all forms of seating removed to make space for the guests, and of course the time scale for these dos was singularly unsatisfactory. Mother liked dinner on the dot of eight o'clock, and would become quite agitated if this routine varied. Cocktails and dinner were not a mix. She judged them to be a socially disastrous American import. In short they were an anathema to her. The cocktail party horror was a theme touched on several times in various articles. Despite this campaign, she was still asked by brave souls to attend them. I cannot recall her ever giving one herself.

Anne liked to give small dinner parties for friends she knew very well. Her work actually gave her all the social life she needed, and at home she preferred to be quiet, indeed often craved it. During her years at the *Sunday Express*, there was little time for dinner parties at home, and the weekends were full too, with gardening and domestics. My father had his friends, and she had hers – and they were not compatible groups. Both socially and in work, they led increasingly separate lives.

The Osbert era heralded a social whirl. He adored company, and loved nothing better than a jolly party, and there were lots. First nights at the Royal Opera House and Glyndebourne (where Osbert designed sets and costumes), grand receptions, parties and dinners. Mother was back on the party circuit with a vengeance. Osbert had the sort of friends that were a delight and a joy to be with. John Betjeman, John Piper, Jock Murray,

Anthony Powell and Moran Caplat were regular visitors. in fact it would be easier to list the people Osbert didn't know, he was the consummate extrovert. Anne was allowed time off for good behaviour as Osbert regularly attended City dinners (apart from the yearly 'ladies' evening' they were always all-male affairs) and ate lunch every day at the Beefsteak or the Garrick. Far from wishing to tag along, Mother would cheer as she packed him off in white tie and tails to some do at the Carpenters' Company and would retire to read, an activity she infinitely preferred. And I cannot imagine that Osbert home for lunch would have been a success; Anne needed to work too. This is from her notebook: 'No woman can work with a man in the house. However keen he is on your income or your interests, he will do anything he can to prevent your concentrating.'

Drinks at home were very acceptable, and a regular occurrence. Often friends and acquaintances would appear for a gin and tonic, or a dry martini – never wine. Snacks were not offered. If we were in the cottage, a bag of crisps might emerge, or in London maybe a peanut, or an olive, but not bulk. In fact Mother rather looked down on those who produced fancy fare, thinking it 'just one more thing to organize'. Guests would arrive 6.30 to 7 o'clock, down two drinks and then it was toes lively, so that everyone could move on with dinner. This was not Anne's invention. It was common protocol, which everyone understood, in a way that they don't seem to now. (When did opening a bottle of wine lead on to become a protracted full-evening event?)

She was at her most social during her life with Osbert. She loved Osbert and Osbert loved parties, so she was prepared to give them her best shot.

In later life, she became less and less interested in social activities. Not that she was antisocial. Anne, like all good journalists, was always interested in gossip, people, and the latest news political or artistic, but she liked a set time frame for these encounters, and always seemed quite relieved when they were over. Giving large dinners always made her nervous, she couldn't just relax and let the evening take over. And she was perfectly content in her own company – happy to take herself off to a restaurant and lunch alone, even more pleased if I turned up unexpectedly and joined her.

Anne admired those people who were party naturals, but was not one. It surprised even her that she had never touched alcohol until she arrived in Fleet Street at the age of forty, when she was won over by a gin and tonic (apparently the corruption was effected by the subs during the hours spent waiting with them in the pub for the proofs of her page). In fact my family seem to down vats of alcohol, at lunch and dinner, in a way that would have me crawling under the table and sobbing were I to emulate them. But I never saw my mother drunk. Osbert was clearly a bit worse for wear after the rounds of port ladled out during his City dinners, but he was a totally benign drunk. I always found his arrival home an entertainment to behold, Mother feigning fury, 'REALLY, OSBERT!', while Osbert, beaming cheerily, would cry 'Dear child! Dear child – a glass of water', before staggering to the bedroom.

HOW OFTEN DO YOU REALLY ASK PEOPLE IN?

This is an attack by me on me. This is an onslaught on my frightful laziness in the matter of inviting our friends to our house. I like shopping. I like cooking. I love seeing people.

We have the space. We have the crocks. We even have the friends.

Yet some strange inhibition comes over me at the thought of *fixing the day*. The idea of dialling some numbers or writing a few letters brings on a paralysis.

So we end up making last-minute dates to lunch or dine in a restaurant, which is twice as dear and half as nice as having people home. Worse still, we end up with an occasional large cocktail party, diabolical invention of the age. Six-thirty seems to me to me the worst possible time for a party.

MOST PEOPLE are tired from a day's work and haven't got their second wind.

SOME PEOPLE are going on to dinner or the movies and have to gallop off in the middle.

THE REST (if the party is a good one, and goes on late) are left hanging around in mid-air around 9 o'clock, primed with drink but unfed, and not knowing what to do about a meal.

Now, this inhospitality isn't

confined to me. I find that hordes of people feel just like I do, wanting, *and intending* to ask more people in more often, but never getting off the mark.

It's a hangover from the war days that has hung on far too long.

'Do you mind if we have dinner out?'
'We don't see half as many people as we used to.'
'Let's meet for lunch.'
'My husband sees people all day, so he doesn't want to be bothered in the evenings'

These are remarks you hear every day, the last one the sad, resigned comment of thousands of stay-at-home women who are lonelier than they know.

And you hear the same excuses abroad. In America, even in France, the restaurant, and the cocktail party, are gaining ground. Yet, when you travel, the invitations you remember with most pleasure and gratitude are the small parties in private houses.

Last week I met two people who really do keep open house.

Both are women who entertain without a lot of money and without much help. In other ways their lives could hardly be more different.

One is a career girl, living in a flat in London on her own. The other is a West Country housewife with a family whose friends are always welcome. Each made me feel strongly that entertaining is a pleasure. Each made me feel it was easy once you've got the habit.

So look out, chums. **Almost any minute you may get asked to dinner.**

26 May 1957

HOW TO MAKE THE GRADE AS A SOCIAL CLIMBER

It's widely agreed that this particular London season is the biggest rat race ever.

So many people seem to be in social difficulties that I thought I'd like to help.

I've spent the week rootling round in society, and have worked out some of the do's and don'ts on How to be a Social Climber.

DO rapidly learn which names to drop. It is widely agreed that most exclusive people in society are the **Oliviers**, so you have to meet them at least once so you can refer to them as Larry and Viv.

DO get on one or two committees for charity balls and rustle up some prizes for the tombola.

Try to see that the ball shows *some* sort of profit for charity – you can't afford a scandal when you're just starting.

DO brush up on your geography of London. Do you know that, as a place to live, stay or entertain in, Mayfair is finished and Belgravia patchy. While Belgrave Square, Chester Square and round and about are still good addresses. Eaton Square is now déclassé; it's too like living in a block of flats. The whole centre of gravity is moving west. My personal bet for the smartest street in London one year from now is out in South Kensington – Pelham Crescent.

DO learn how to spend your money. You simply can't go wrong with a racehorse. To own some decent bloodstock and let fall a tip or two will win you a seat at any dinner table in the land.

DO get asked to a lunch party by one of the following: the American, French or Spanish Ambassador, Sir Chips Channon, or Lady Pamela Berry. These are as high as you can go.

DO learn the customs about clothes and food. For instance, you can wear quite awful clothes so long as you have a tiara. You can serve really filthy food so long as it comes on Crown Derby and you lay on a good martini first. This should consist of gin and ice.

BE CAUTIOUS

While you should be cautious about British journalists and broadcasters, you can give of your best to their American brothers. Where you would hesitate to invite Robin Day or Richard Dimbleby, ask Art Buchwald or Ed Murrow. On no account ask me.

NOTES
Sir Henry Channon, known as 'Chips' (1897–1958) An American-born British Conservative politician, author and diarist.
Lady Pamela Berry (1914–1982) Society hostess and wife of Michael Berry (Lord Hartwell), press baron, who took over the *Daily Telegraph* in 1954
Robin Day (1923–2000) Political broadcaster and commentator. Renowned for his ability to cross-question politicians, he changed the face of television debate.
Richard Dimbleby (1913–1965) English journalist and broadcaster, leading news commentator, and host of the flagship current affairs programme *Panorama*.
Art Buchwald (1925–2007) American humorist and columnist for *The Washington Post*.
Ed Murrow (1908–1965) American TV journalist and news broadcaster for CBS.
Robert Edwards (1925–2012) Journalist who was to enter the *Guinness Book of Records* as 'The Fleet Street editor who has worked on the most titles'.

7 July 1957

TAPPED AT THE PARTY

Have you played my new party game? It's called Telephones I Would Like To Tap. This fine new game is pushing even the TV set into the background as entertainment.

In the simplest version, you can just see who can think up the telephone lines likeliest to produce the fruitiest conversations.

For instance, I'd like to cut in on: **Prince Philip talking to his motor insurance company.**

But at really spirited parties two guests assume the roles of two people on the telephone, and some of the conversations are so dazzling that soon, no doubt, there will be some nasty writs for slander.

I wish I could tell you in full the conversation I heard acted out which began 'Hello, Hugh darling, this is me.' But if there is one thing I am fussy about, it's keeping out of the courts.

The joy of this improving game is that you can apply it to any circle.

At a Fleet Street party you could have Robert Edwards consulting his solicitor.

In educational circles, the headmaster of Charterhouse talking to the headmaster of Eton.

Anyway try it yourself at a party, or to while away a journey. Uproarious laughter guaranteed.

GIVE THAT DO-IT-YOURSELF PARTY THE LUXURY TOUCH

Draw the curtains, light the lamps, and swing from the chandelier, because it's time to give a party. Summer's gone, travellers are home, the autumn crackles with frost outside and hospitality within.

It **does not crackle**, heaven be praised, with the brittle jollity of cocktail parties. This poisonous form of entertainment – nothing to eat, nowhere to sit, chirruping from person to person on an empty stomach – is dying on its feet.

The only cocktail party cards I've got on my shelf at the moment are two for business binges, one to launch a new mouthwash and one to celebrate a new method of welding angle brackets.

Gay? I'll say so. Instead of cocktails, anyone who can read a recipe, hire a cook, or select with skill from the delicatessen, is giving dinner parties. And notice the plural. The habit is back of entertaining a few people frequently, easily, and as a matter of course. Six months lethargy followed by a guilty kill-off of eighty people will no longer do.

KEY IDEAS

I've been talking to some of the well-known party people who are adept at the single-handed dinner party.

Terence and Shirley Conran are giving a party for four. The menu: avocados with shrimp mayonnaise; *foie de porc braisé*, mashed potatoes, two salads; cold grapefruit soufflé; 2 bottles of Mâcon.

David Knight, handsome American star of *The Young Lovers*, is giving a party for eight: melon; American meatloaf, baked potatoes, salad; baked Alaska pudding; *vin rosé*.

THEY AGREE on candlelight for its glamour. But extra lighting as well, 'so you can see clearly what you are picking at'.

THEY AGREE on tablecloths. Everything was suggested from tartan linen to pink organdie, though for a formal party white damask is still best beloved. Even the prettiest mats do not dress the table enough.

THEY AGREE that you must learn to pick good inexpensive wines *vin rosé*, Mâcon, the light Austrian white wines. For six people perhaps one bottle of white and two of red, rather than three the same.

THEY AGREE that flowers are a mistake on the table. Unless your flowers are kept low and small they get in the way. If you need a centrepiece, most prefer a group of candles or a dish of fruit.

THEY AGREE on the importance of the way each dish looks, and of the dish you serve it in. For instance, lovely casseroles that come from oven to the table. Black pottery dishes for butter. Baskets for bread or toast. Cheese served on straw. Silver must be beautifully polished. But food itself should never be overdecorated – 'garnished but not Technicolor'.

NOTE
Terence Conran British designer. In 1953 he opened his first business, The Soup Kitchen. Married Shirley Conran in 1954. Their opinions on food, interiors and lifestyle set the bar.

Mum and me, 1952.

Anne and Mothering

Mother did put her career over family life, but we were well cared for by a selfless group of individuals who could be relied on to put us at the heart of the house. She passed on very little in terms of actual instruction. Anne did not stand by me at the kitchen table schooling me in the art of folding fairy cakes, or issue me with a trowel for planting up a pot, I can't recall a knitting or make-up demonstration, a tennis lesson or indeed any insight into the arts or literature. The whole rearing process relied on my observation and a maternal osmosis, but in the end that is probably the best way. You choose the bits you want to retain and discard the rest.

Anne would have been miserable without her work. She had worked hard to forge a career in those testosterone times and wasn't going to give it up. Nor would I have wanted her to. I was very conscious of her achievements. I learnt from Anne that work was immensely fulfilling, and could provide comfort in times of stress. Her work ethic was extraordinary, and it fed into me. She was the ideal role model for a daughter. It never occurred to me that women might be considered by some to be a subspecies, I assumed that men and women were equal, which is a very useful starting point when you leave the nest.

Was Anne a 'good' mother? She certainly wasn't a physical parent. Anne had perfected the art of a one-cheek air kiss, and had never got to grips with the concept of hugging. She was absolutely hopeless at expressing her love for her children – to whom she was completely devoted, I had to work hard to discover the emotions she felt. Anne's own oppressive childhood had left its mark. She was also so desperate not to be any sort of burden that she went to the opposite pole.

Anne taught me resilience. She was quite alarming in a good many ways. I was acutely aware of her beauty and talents and I was also receptive to her moods. I grew up wanting to please. There were too many disparate factions in our family and I dreaded confrontation from any of them. The result is, I really don't dwell on gloomy. I always now feel rather sorry for children who have had the 'perfect childhood'. When life comes from left field, as it inevitably will, I have noticed that as adults they lack coping mechanisms. My mechanism is well oiled.

We shared a sense of humour, which is say a strong appreciation of irony. I could catch her eye and know exactly what she was thinking. She could also be very disruptive in situations that normally required solemn and steady attention. At church, at school assemblies, or on any sort of pompous occasion, I would absolutely have to avoid looking at her, or she could set me off with a couple of words, or a hum-along. In old age, when she became slightly deaf, she also became more fearless, and would say things out loud, thinking no one could hear, which would set me off in a slightly different way.

Mother could spring into action if required. Never judgmental when it came to my personal relationships, she was an excellent ally when one came to an end, providing practical support – or sometimes wading in, if she felt it appropriate – but she knew instinctively when to stand back. Anne realized from her own life that you have to kiss a few frogs. She was always generous financially, worrying about my bank balance, my lack of holidays and the conspicuous absence of domestic back-up. Snap.

As a teenager I was included in all social gatherings, and I realized very early on what a privilege that was. To associate with individuals who were simply brilliant in their field. I really did marvel at their depth of knowledge, talent and *joie de vivre*. How could you not? Betjeman, the Pipers, the Powells, the Murrays, Moran Caplat, George Malcolm Thompson, Roy Strong . . . the list goes on and on. Home life was anything but boring. I also came to realize that celebrity is fleeting, and even those with gifted and gilded lives are forgotten surprisingly quickly.

I also knew that I was essential to Anne's well-being. After Osbert became ill, I was probably the only person she really wanted to see. I provided the moments of relief in an otherwise choppy sea. I had replaced her brother John as her trusted support and friend.

So, the perfect mother? Well, obviously, there were times I would happily have left her in the supermarket and attached myself to another, more homely, body, but I would have realized the error of my ways by the time we reached the car. I am of course, in the end – with a few kinks along the way – my mother's daughter, and of that I am very proud.

23 September 1956

CHILDREN: TRUTH VERSUS TACT

I went for four days holiday to Spain, leaving my reputation in the worst possible hands – my children's.

When I'm out, my son likes to answer the phone.

He told photographer John French, 'Well she's due back today, but I don't suppose for a moment she'll turn up. You know what she is.'

He told my mother-in-law, 'Is there any chance of coming to tea with you, Granny? There's not a thing in the house to eat.'

He told a business magnate I've been trying to impress, 'There are piles of bills on the hall table, and she's forgotten my pocket money.'

At what age do children acquire that splendid virtue which so far transcends truth and honesty – tact ?

UNEMOTIONAL

I had been watching a documentary about absentee parents and neglected children. By the end, it had me worried. 'Do I neglect you?' I asked my son, 'Do you feel unwanted? Lacking in security? Driven to seek unsuitable companions? Would you rather I stayed at home and looked after you all or that I went on working and we had help at home?'

'Much better you work,' he said. 'The more money comes into the house the better.'

In our family it never pays to be dewy-eyed.

21 October 1956

NEVER UNDERESTIMATE THE POWER OF THE CHILD

For ten short little years out of several million, Britain has been a woman's country.

'You women are so important,' men keep telling us. 'Just look at your spending power – why, we daren't do a thing without consulting you. When we advertise our goods, it's *you* we talk to.

'At elections, it's *your* vote we're after. When we make motor cars we paint them pretty colours to attract *your* custom. We never make a film without a love story because we know *you* choose the shows.'

Well, *our* reign didn't last long did it?

Because Britain is becoming a child's country just as fast as it takes to say Davy Crockett. More and more goods, more and more advertising, more and more films, more and more books and newspapers are being angled at the young consumer.

'Young James', says the advertisement, 'has never once regretted advising his father to buy a new Austin.'

Twenty years ago, Dad would have taken the advice of that mechanical genius in the office. Two years ago he would have asked his wife what car *she* wanted. But now Dad gets talked into a car by a kid of twelve.

MEMO TO CAR MEN

Dear, clever motor manufacturers, why have you got it into your heads that what a woman looks for in a car is a nice pretty colour?

Who cares about two-tone pastel shades? Not me.

All I ask of a car is that at the touch of a wonder button, it will move sideways and park itself neatly in its own length.

I'M FOND OF CHILDREN, BUT . . . THIS CULT OF MOTHER'S EARTH!

I'm fond of children and I like babies, but the way women go on about childbirth is beginning to put me off both.

My gorge rises at the new cult of Mother Earth. The pendulum has swung from prudery to exhibitionism, so that no expectant mother seems to be happy unless she is writing about her experiences in the newspapers or having a baby on TV. While the really lucky ones have the whole business recorded so that they can play it back whenever they like.

There are many aspects of the Mother Earth cult, some, no doubt, scientifically desirable.

One of the weirder ones is the idea that fathers ought to take a much bigger share than they usually do in pregnancy. More and more expectant fathers now do preparatory exercises with their wives. Some go along to the hospital for the event and give the midwives a helping hand.

(I always used to feel sorry for the bus conductors who have to weigh in when thoughtless babies arrive in the bus, but now I think I've been wasting my sympathy.)

Another tenet of the cult which I mistrust is the theory that as childbirth is a natural process, it can be accompanied painlessly without anaesthetic.

Now, here I know I am on treacherous ground. I know women who swear by childbirth by relaxation, and some good doctors who support it. On the other hand I have known women who have expected babies by this method with complete confidence and have had the shock of their lives.

What make me suspicious of it is the mumbo-jumbo that goes with it.

In the first place there is a lot of silly talk about nature knowing best. Nature may (*possibly*) have known best five thousand years ago, but does she now? Would the doctors who crack up Nature prefer a raw hunk of reindeer gnawed with the teeth or a grilled steak with béarnaise sauce eaten with a knife and fork and mustard?

Even phonier, to my mind, is the quasi-religious language in which some of the new theories are described.

'The fearless woman', writes Dr Grantly Dick Read, 'advances to the dais of the Almighty to receive the prize for her accomplishment. She does not cringe in anticipation of admonition, but is proud and grateful for her just reward.'

What does this drivel mean? I swear that any woman who spends nine months with a goofy look on her face brooding about her inside is every bit as maladjusted as the poor, ignorant Victorian woman who spent the time dreading her punishment for sin.

I think that, while welcoming science, one should conduct one's life with a certain amount of *taste*. And that Mother Earth is an ugly, galumphing sort of deity, who lacks taste, humour and common sense.

WHY SHE'S HAVING HER BABY AT HOME

I find that more and more women are choosing to have their babies in natural surroundings. It used to be a privilege to have a baby in a hospital. Now it's a privilege to have them at home.

Antonia Pakenham – now Mrs Hugh Fraser – who is expecting a baby in June, has given me some splendid reasons why.

'First,' she says, 'I'd like my husband to know it's happening. If I go off for ten days in June to a sacred female shrine with priestesses, he'll only have my word for it that I've had a baby at all.

'So far he's quite detached from it. I'd like him at least to hear the shrieks.

'Then, I'm looking forward immensely to the time afterwards. I want it to be the supreme moment of my life. I'm very healthy and never get the chance to go to bed, and I intend to remain bedridden for as long as the doctor will allow. I shall order a trousseau of bedjackets and I shan't get up till they're worn out. If it's sunny I shall be wheeled to the balcony for air. I meant to order some beautiful outdoor furniture until I discovered the price. And I shall have hundreds of visitors – far more than any hospital would allow.'

'Have you got any feelings about it, medically speaking?' I asked.

'Yes, strong ones. I associate hospitals with illness, and this isn't an illness at all. Though I understand a mother with a big family or with no help preferring hospital as a rest from the household. I think it will be nice not having to worry whether the baby arrives on time or early or late. It must be such a bore waiting with the car at the ready and one's drum on top of the wardrobe. I also think it will be better for the eldest child when one has a second. As you know I am the eldest of eight, and I'd have hated it if Mother had disappeared and come back with a horrible bundle in her arms. As it was, I took the other children as a matter of course.

'By the way, I was a no-love baby myself. I was born when the theory was in fashion that a baby must never be picked up, or kissed, or fed before its time. Mother dropped all that for the other seven. By rights I ought to have been a juvenile delinquent. But we all seem to have turned out much the same.'

Admiring Mrs Fraser's beauty – she looked as chic as a model in a plain black suit – and listening to her radiant plans, I felt that the no-love baby had turned out pretty well. And that the baby-at-home would land (metaphorically) on its feet.

NOTE
Antonia Fraser, née Pakenham Author and historian. Eldest daughter of Lord Longford. Married 1956 Conservative MP Sir Hugh Fraser, with whom she had six children. The Frasers were divorced in 1977 and in 1980 she married Harold Pinter (who died in 2008).

POSTSCRIPT

WHEN WILL A HUSBAND SHOP AND LIKE IT?

I've been talking to a woman with blissfully refreshing views: Mrs Hugh Fraser (Antonia Pakenham), who has just had a baby.

Mrs Fraser was bright enough to have her baby six weeks early, and so jockeyed her husband into doing all the shopping.

'Not a thing was ready,' she told me. 'No pram and practically no layette. I'd got the bare cradle but none of the trimmings. My husband had to rush out and buy – everything – matinee jackets, baby powder, baby nightgowns and masses of things for me. It worked very well. I must say, he has an excellent taste in bootees.'

Full marks

'In fact I give him full marks as a shopper. He even bought me a pair of earrings, only he was so excited he left them in a taxi.' (Happy postscript, they came back.)

I think this idea of leaving half the shopping undone is rather brilliant; other young mothers might copy.

It sort of catches a man in a vulnerable moment . . . the one time in his life when he'll do your shopping without one murmur of complaint.

17 March 1957

WARNING – TO MOTHERS

When they invented psychiatrists for dogs I thought the Americans had reached their limit. But no.

The new idea is for children to psychoanalyse their parents. A well-known writer in the American magazine *Seventeen* advises teenagers on how to help their crazy, mixed-up mothers.

These are quotes from the current number.

'Try to build up your mother's faith in herself, as a mother and as a person.'

'Have you ever really asked her how she met your father?'

'Few women – even mothers – can resist telling about past emotional experiences to a really sympathetic listener.'

'From what you've told us about your mother, we wonder whether, right now, you *could* make her understand all that this means to you.'

Well I hereby give warning to all children within my orbit . . .

THAT IF I catch you eyeing me quizzically, wondering if I'm insecure **OR IF** I catch you boring into my past **OR IF** I find you entering sympathetically into my interests and making me feel I'm loved and wanted **. . . I'll readjust our relationship with a damned good smack.**

THOSE PILLS – CHILDREN TOO

It's the last straw. I find that children have been asking for pep pills to help them through the end - of - term exams.

Soon toddlers will need Vitality Pills to help them face the horrors of the ABC.

Boarding school children will want Readjustment Pills before they can face the holidays and the turmoil of family life.

Adolescents will take Happiness Pills to get them through those difficult years.

Babies with need Courage Pills before they can face a ride in a pram.

I am appalled at the way we are passing on this horrible habit to the younger generation.

Bring me a pill someone. I'm off to meet the school train.

5 May 1957

WHAT A WONDERFUL HOLIDAY – NEXT TIME I'LL GO TO SIBERIA

So it's goodbye to the dear, gay school holidays and the tranquil pleasures of family life. It's pleasant to recall how one sweet, romping day succeeded another.

Take the first week with our little lot . . .

That was the week when my son caught the mumps and the other children staying in the house were hurriedly withdrawn in closed carriages by reproachful parents.

When my daughter fell in the river (Father was in charge) and ran a temperature of 105 while the house was tense with recriminations.

When the stove got in a mood and I couldn't get the oven hot.

When 250 rose bushes and sweet pea plants, ordered in January, arrived in a crate with a note advising immediate planting.

Take the second pleasure-laden week . . .

That was the week of the thrush's funeral. **When** there was a sad little coffin and a funeral cortège and a tombstone movingly inscribed 'May his little soul rest happy' and some good singing and everyone crying like mad.

Crocodile's tears really, because of course the children had murdered the bird. Convinced that they were St Francis of Assisi and St Joan respectively ('Even the wild creatures would come and sit in her lap'), they had been unsuccessfully rearing nestlings near the kitchen stove. Left to itself, that fluffy chick would have lived to steal my strawberries in July.

It was the week when the budgerigar got and out and the car conked and we got a meaningless but disquieting bill from the income tax.

Take the third week . . .

That was the week my daughter got mumps and I had to cancel seats for *The Entertainer* (there aren't any more), and when my son fell out of a tree (pushed, some say), and my husband hopped it for the Continent.

When my best friends arrived on a flying visit from abroad, and I was stuck in the country, and they had a marvellous week without me.

That was the week of too many Easter eggs eaten by too

Me - just loving Frinton.

few people, with punishing conse-quences.

Take the fourth, climactic week of this idyllic season . . .

That was the week when I went to London and got mumps ('Can you beat it, our beauty queen's mumpy,' my son reported laconically), and I wondered why people with small pig eyes in large criminal faces bother to live.

When I kept getting up and posting cabbages to the country contingent, because in the country there's a chronic shortage of fresh vegetables – it's only in towns that you get a good healthy assortment.

When I had a breeze with the office, who couldn't see why I couldn't interview lots of sparkling people while running a temperature of 101 – 'only don't come near *us*,' they said.

'What about the sparkling people?' I said. 'They may not want it either.' 'Find someone who's had the thing,' they suggested. 'That narrows the field,' I said crossly, and went back to bed.

When my son took my daughter, well wrapped up, on a ten-minute convalescent stroll in the sun, and brought her home stumbling blindly, two hours later, gloves, cap and muffler gone.

'We went a little too far,' he explained. 'For the last two miles, I had to prop her eyelids open with matchsticks to keep her awake.'

When I had to check the school clothing list of eighty-six items.

Yes, they've been wonderful, enchanting holidays, though I use the word 'holiday' with a merry laugh.

For sheer relaxation, all I ask, now I'm free, is to be sent on a juicy assignment to Siberia.

HOLIDAY QUOTES

'Oh goodie, plastic tablecloths.'
'Mother, can I shove her under?'
'I think I've had enough cream.'
'Quick! Quick! The first aid box.'
'We'll eat our lunch in the lion house.'
'I think it's dead.'
'Come on, it's lovely and cold in the sea.'

Anne walking down the road in front
of her cottage.

Anne and Domestics

I cannot remember Mother making a bed; sometimes she would pull over the odd sheet, but certainly no hospital corners. She toyed with idea of washing-up, but was of the school that believes a tea towel is there to 'finish the job off'. Dusting and general cleaning were not a consideration.

Despite not doing much herself, Mother was keen to make sure I knew the basics – or what she considered the basics. One of her favourite how-tos was to inform me on the intricacies of cleaning picture glass. 'Now, look, dear, I was shown how to do this by a *very* good art dealer, who *really* knew his stuff. Only put the *smallest* squeeze of cleaner on the glass . . . NO, too much . . .' Mother was keen on an expert.

Anne certainly did a bit of cooking, mostly in the country, but never the shopping. In my youth everything was 'on account', and delivered. In London Harrods was the grocer of choice, in the country the small village shop would supply the necessities, delivered to the back door on a Saturday morning by Ted, who was the cheeriest soul ever known, announcing his presence by whistling his way up the garden path,

There is no doubt that Anne would have found working life a lot harder if she had run the household with the aid only of a recalcitrant au pair. Luckily, she didn't have to.

We had no modern appliances, they didn't exist, but we did have plenty of 'hands'. The number of people arriving to take care of our really very small household would be considered on a par to the staff requirements of a start-up company today.

I should also say, I don't think we were what would have been considered a rich family. However, in the early fifties both my parents were very good earners. My mother's take-home pay was £3,000 a year, later increasing as rivals started to bid for her talents .My father's career took a dive in the late fifties, when Anne was relied on to keep the various ships afloat. Our flats were always rented, not bought. Neither parent had any inheritance as backup. Indeed, the only time when my mother felt financially secure was when she married my stepfather, which allowed her to relax from the monthly grind. All that said, Anne had a substantial pay roll, which I don't think would be possible today on a journo's wage.

In London there was Nanny, who lived with us and loved her charges too much ever to consider a holiday apart (if she went back home to visit relatives in Sheffield my brother and I would often go too). Nanny, Jessie Strafford, was from the old school of child care. I could write a whole book on Nanny, who had been in service since the age of fourteen. I learnt my first and, sadly, only words in Swahili on Nanny's knee: 'Jambo! Leta chai upesi, upesi', a vital phrase in the nursery lexicon, meaning 'Hello! Bring tea quickly, quickly.' And you must say 'upesi' twice. Nanny pronounced it 'pacee'. Nanny had worked for Lord Denham, who had been Governor-General in Kenya, before she arrived to slum it with us. Nanny was pretty old even when she first arrived for the birth of my brother in 1948. The idea had been that she would stay until my brother left to go to prep school, but in 1951 I was born, and Nanny was once again in demand.

She remained until I was twelve, only leaving when I could no longer cope with the level of care she still wished to provide. I went to a day school in Sloane Square, and by the time I was ten Nanny was too old to manage public transport, so the same black cab, cognisant of timings, would drive by every morning, stopping outside the flat to pick us up.

We nearly always had tea at Peter Jones on Sloane Square. We had our special table by the window, and the staff knew what we liked – a selection of sandwiches and a pot of tea. Nanny did the 'pools' and studied the 'shares', doing rather well at both. She would ask my advice on draws and goals, although I had not the slightest idea what we were doing. She was a fan of premium bonds too. I have to say it was Nanny who really brought me up. Anne was often away on assignments, or working late. Holidays to the cottage, Frinton and once Butlin's (my brother got nits, so we didn't go *there* again), were all taken in Nanny's care. When, after eighteen years, she eventually retired, it was to a hotel on the Cromwell Road, her life reduced to another small room in a home that would never be her own. She left me a small gold and sapphire engagement ring in her will. In all those years I never knew the name of her fiancé. I can only assume that he died, like so many young men, in the First World War. She taught me 'It's a Long, Long Way to Tipperary', which I remember singing with gusto on the bus when I was small.

Mrs Elsie Elmer, our daily, came every weekday, arriving at 7.30 a.m. to prepare my mother's breakfast (Earl Grey tea and a triangle of Hovis, delivered in bed on a tray along with all the morning papers), before cleaning the flat, sorting the washing, etc., to leave around lunchtime.

Mrs Elmer was whip-thin and never stopped. Nanny tried to lord it over her, without much success. Elsie's son, Bobby, had 'done well', and emigrated to Australia with his family, which was a real sadness to her, as her husband had died and she lived in very poor circumstances in Shepherd's Bush. Happily, when Elsie eventually left us Bobby sent for her. She boarded her first plane and retired to live with the family in Perth. I went to her house for the first and last time to say goodbye, a week before she left. There, on top of her suitcase, packed for the journey, was an old teddy in a polythene bag. 'Did I think they would let teddy in?' Elsie had heard that everything in Australia was very new and clean, and maybe they would stop him at the border. I am delighted to report that both Elsie and teddy made it through, and their well deserved retirement was an extremely happy one.

In the late fifties, our culinary life took a leap with the arrival of Martha Todd, our cook. Martha arrived at 9.30 a.m. ready to receive instructions and prepare lunch and tea, leaving at around 4 p.m., with dinner ready to rock. If there were guests, then Martha would stay on to cook, serve and clear.

On Friday afternoon we decamped to the cottage. Nanny usually came to the cottage, and there was always a gardener for lawn mowing, digging or constructing 'a proper erection' (Mother unwittingly mentioned these last words on a gardening radio show, unaware of the innuendo; all the more pronounced as the phrase had barely left her lips before the interviewer called time, up came the music and her last words were left suspended in the ether). Weekend cleaning, fire laying, floor polishing and washing-up were done initially by Mrs Dobson, who lived across the road and also helped with the cooking,. Later these tasks were taken on by Mrs Mansell (Phyllis), who didn't do cooking, but took care of Mother's dachshund, Maud, during the week.

Proper cleaning was achieved when we were back in town. Friday was the day to 'open up' and make sure everything was tickety-boo for our arrival. Saturday morning around 10 a.m. Mrs Mansell would come in for bed-making and general tidying, Sunday morning ditto. We returned to town on Sunday afternoon, to prepare for the week, leaving the washing-up from lunch to be completed in our absence.

Anne must have been an excellent employer, as nobody (apart from Mrs Dobson, who was seen off by my brother's shenanigans) ever left. They all stayed for decades, vital cogs in our domestic wheel, allowing Anne to get on with other stuff.

When I look back, it seems utterly extraordinary that there was enough for them all to do, but they never stopped working. It also strikes me as odd that I have managed to fit in work at all without this level of back-up. Still, watching others toil and cook for my entire youth honed my skills in the domestic field to quite a superior level. I am the Queen of Clean and absolutely at home with the range.

NANNY

Nurse Lightbody – soon to leave Buckingham Palace – has worked so long for Royalty that she can never have come up against the normal facts of life. For instance, I don't suppose the Duke of Gloucester or the Duke of Edinburgh ever touched her for a fiver.

There are perhaps fifty thousand nannies left in Britain, but few of them still live in the Lightbody style to which they were once accustomed.

Most of them fit in now with irregular characters like me.

Our nanny was once the Lightbody type. She was boss of the nurseries at Government House, Nairobi, with a squad of coloured boys to help her turn East Africa into a honey-for-tea extension of England.

But, like the Brigade of Guards, she has kept up with the times. She is equally successful now as a nurse-financier-houskeeper-tele-phonist-cook-bottlewasher.

TOO DISCREET

SHE advises us on all Stock Exchange matters, on which she is an expert. She never believes that I own no stocks and shares, as '*everyone* has stocks and shares, you know.'

SHE is a great help with the football pools. (*Remember Evelyn Waugh's Nanny Bloggs, who 'always brought off a few showy doubles in the flat-racing season'?*)

SHE is a mine of inside information about the Royal tours (she *lived* in Government House) and the Royal house-hold (*she knew weeks before that Nanny Lightbody had given notice, but was too discreet to tell me*).

SHE is the adored confidante of my children. My son, away at school, found out last week that he had run up a bill for 1*s.* 6*d.* at a Chelsea toyshop.

'*Sell some of my toys,*' he wrote to her, '*and raise the money somehow. Get across London at all costs and pay the bill. Destroy this letter.*'

SHE is my stand-in for a hundred jobs whenever I go away. My gratitude is only marred by the relish with which she announces bad news on my return.

On my last three trips I have been met by Nanny saying in a voice of doom:

'Your daughter has been running a fever of 104.'

'Your husband was carried away in an ambulance on Tuesday night.'

'I'm afraid there's been a shooting incident.'

I now counter the attack by getting my question in first. I ring up from the airport and bark down the phone: 'I'm back, who's hurt?'

SHE is a wizard with the cash box. When nobody else has a bean to pay a taxi or go to the cinema, she whistles up a pound or two from a cache which (not for want of trying) I have never been able to uncover.

I suppose Nurse Lightbody (or, more correctly, Nanny Windsor) has never enjoyed any of this knockabout side of family life. She can never have had to fork out for a taxi fare or muck in with the cooking.

If she had – the Queen could never bear to part with her.

6 October 1957

THAT SOUNDS LIKE MUMMY SHOUTING

I have often wondered how it is that people get murdered within a few yards of sane, normal, kindly citizens. Now I know.

An American portrait painter came home to have a drink and talk business. I have never met him before. He is charming. We chat politely. Then, as he is due at the theatre, he gets up to go.

But the door has irrevocably locked itself, and we can't get out. We bash at it and yell through the keyhole, but Nanny is bathing my daughter and doesn't hear, and there's nobody else at home.

'The telephone?' says my friend.

'It's not in this room,' I reply.

'Your husband?' he says.

'He won't be home till nine.'

At this point my friend eyes me suspiciously, by no means sure I have not fixed the lock, or that I have a husband at all. It could be a frame-up.

We now try the window. A long drop. The street is rainy and deserted, except for two Indian gentlemen at whom we wave and shout frantically. With the sagacity of their race they cotton on, plunge into the building, and send the porter up to open the door.

Sunny smiles all round. My friend will at least get to the theatre for the second act.

But it was Nanny who delivered the *coup de grâce*.

'What a funny thing,' she said. 'I said to Clare, when I was washing her ears, "Why, that sounds just like Mummy shouting."'

'What a funny thing,' I said. 'It was.'

Our nanny, Jessie Strafford, at the
start of her career. Needless to say,
those sailor-suited angels are not us.

Proof that birthday teas really were
rather sensational.

Anne and Children's Parties

It has to be said that Anne, for whom children in bulk might well have been – to put it mildly – a trial, really came into her own when giving a children's party. Everything was planned down to the last balloon, and a really good time was had by all – especially Nanny, who could bask in pride as her charges took centre stage.

The teas were a wonder to behold. Large glass jugs filled with lemon and orange squash, plates heaving with small sandwiches (no crusts), biscuits in piles, jellies that wobbled and blocks of Wall's ice cream (this was served after the main tea, on trays, half an hour before going home). A themed birthday cake with your name was delivered by Harrods and gold spindly chairs were hired in, along with the tables, which were linked together and covered in white cloths. Everyone in the class was asked, and we all had our special party frocks. Mine was a red and white nylon affair. To die for.

Sometimes we had an entertainer. One, Mr Ernest Castro, was the equivalent of today's Sharky & George. If Mr Castro didn't come you were dead in the water. This was, I am sorry to say, not because of his undoubted talents as a magician, but because he had developed an entertainment which involved the party girl 'getting married'. This was the 1950s. All your friends played the minor roles – the bridegroom, the bridesmaids, guests, etc., and were dressed up accordingly in top hats and carried large bouquets of feather flowers, but – here's the crunch – only the birthday girl could ever be **the bride**. Only **the bride** could wear *the* wedding ring, a glittering tiara, a veil and – this was the real humdinger – go inside the silver foil coach which Mr Castro would whirl and twirl around the drawing room. She (I) was Cinderella. It was intoxicating. This clever contrivance meant that Mr Castro was pretty much guaranteed to be booked twenty-three more times to repeat his show. All twenty-four little girls just had to get their hands on that gold ring and lord it up in the coach. He also had a puppet – a hideous wooden schoolgirl called Lettice Leefe, complete with long black plaits and a St Trinian's-style uniform. She sang a jolly song, and, again, the birthday girl was central. Mr Castro gave me a recording of the song on a brittle 78 (long gone, sadly).

I'm Lettice Leefe, oh jolly dee,
There's not another girl like me.
My best intentions come to grief,
There's no one quite like Lettice Leefe.
La di da de da, La di da de dee.

It was a winner.

Yes, Mr Castro was a master in child psychology, he knew how to get the bookings. What did he do to entertain boys? Maybe he didn't and the juvenile brides guaranteed he had enough work to fill his calendar.

I do not remember Anne ever having a party disaster. They were planned and thought through from arrival to departure (obviously with balloons, prizes, and a 'going home' present). Before the arrival of the entertainer there might be 'progressive

The silver foil coach. Sad but true, this remains one of my life's highlights.

games'. These took place on small card tables, and you might have, say, ten minutes to create a fancy dress outfit out of crepe paper (pins and scissors were not then a health and safety issue), before Anne would ring a little bell to signal dashing on to the next table for another game. Mother would have invented and sorted all the tables herself, I don't think Nanny would have had the imagination, being much happier managing the tea table, and supervising hand-washing. All the traditional classics were played too – musical chairs, pass the parcel, pin the tail on the donkey, etc.

My father kept his distance from these all-female events. He did come once, towards the end of the afternoon and, turning off all the lights, caused mayhem and joy by shining a torch in his mouth, so his cheeks and eyes lit up like a ghoul as he pursued us up the corridor making peculiar noises. Happy Days!

Boys will be boys. A party set up for *Picture Post* – sadly, the participants lost the plot.

YOU ARE MONTGOMERY AND THIS IS ALAMEIN

A children's party is either a wow or a flop – no halfway house. Having given, in my life as a mother, one flop and five wows, I claim to know the secret of the thing. **You must treat it as a military operation.** 'What shall we do now?' are words of doom. PERFECT YOUR PLANS many days before *the* day (you are Montgomery and this is Alamein).

CHOOSE YOUR STAFF for their youth and strength. For a party of twenty-four small boys you will need four to six adults who *know they have come to work*. Turn down the well-meant offers of aunts, godmothers and grannies, who want to watch the fun. Having to be polite to them is a distraction you can't afford.

TIME YOUR PARTY to the split second. (Personally, I think a short, sharp party is better than a three-hour test of endurance.)

Remember that children, unlike adults, *always arrive early*. You should be ready with hair brushed, ribbons tied, etc., fifteen minutes in advance.

We always give each guest a balloon on arrival (some prefer to give them on departure); get 33.5 per cent extra to allow for bursts.

Between zero hour and tea you need a programme of games that children can join on to as they arrive.

It is impossible to overestimate the rapaciousness of children over six. If tea comes at 4.30 sharp, time the second half of the assault to start at 5.0 – tea won't spin out for more than half an hour. Young children are too excited to eat much; older ones gobble.

At 5.00 comes the main entertainment – and it had better be good. If you are rich and lazy you will have a conjurer or a film show. (Don't fall into the trap of forgetting that children mature. The children who were tickled pink by the conjurer when they were five will die of ennui now they are six.)

At 5.45 a lot should happen. Trays should come on with ice cream. More trays should come on with a present for each guest. And the doorbell should start ringing as parents come to collect.

Offer the parents sherry, and sherry only. I once found my husband mixing a different gin drink for each parent, which meant he was perfectly useless for getting taxis.

In the case of children's parties I have a motto corny enough for a cracker: 'Money isn't everything.'

Parties in the richest houses are often the worst. It's your blood and sweat that will win the day.

NOTE WRITTEN A YEAR LATER

I didn't tell you at the time, but one of my famous Systems came completely unstuck this time last year.

I refer to my theory that you must treat a small boys' party as a military operation, making your plans with clockwork accuracy. It had always worked before but last year the battle got out of hand. The boys went berserk.

Lamps were smashed, cakes thrown, parlour fireworks ground into the carpet.

This year I'm trying new tactics. I'm introducing a softening influence in the shape of girls. One of two things will happen . . . either the party will be decorous and successful . . . or the girls will be pounded to pulp. *I wonder which.*

Maud, our long-haired dachshund.

Anne and Pets

Anne felt about pets the same way she felt about children. She liked some. Actually, not very many. She was always considerate to them, but really thought it would be much better if fewer people owned them – including my father, who was often referred to as 'the animal murderer'. In fact during my childhood, I can in all honesty say that not many pets would have cheered at being brought into our household.

The smaller ones – budgies and hamsters – were purchased, along with everything else deemed vital to life, from Harrods. All our budgies were brilliantly named 'Chirpy', which they were when they arrived. They were always blue, so really it was quite hard to tell the new from the old. One learnt to say 'Pretty boy' and was allowed out to fly round the nursery, where he would alight on the top of the curtain rails, staring down and nibbling at the edges of the pelmet. At the sight of fresh seed he would nip back home to his cage, where he could be watched splashing in his little plastic bath, or bashing away at his mirror and bell. It was, of course, only a matter of time before the window was left open and Chirpy made a dash for the freedom of the Earls Court Road. Cue for wailing and tears, and a lot of walking up and down the side streets plaintively calling out his name.

He chose not to return.

As we got slightly older, we were allowed hamsters. My brother had one called Snowy, and there were also Weeny and Goldilocks. We understood very early on in the proceedings that hamsters are hopeless at sharing, Snowy suffering a nasty nip around the eye from Weeny, as first off they were allowed to cohabit. Remarkably quickly, instead of one cage we had three. These stood on top of a long, narrow bookcase in the hall. The game of choice was pulling strips from the ivy print wallpaper, which they could just access with a bit of effort by squashing up their noses and forcing their hideous yellow incisors through the bars. I tried to hide this habit by judiciously sliding the cage along to cover the holes, which just meant they had a new area to decimate.

They often escaped, running amok around the flat, nibbling soft furnishings, and taking tufts from the red carpet to line their nests. Once, during a night-time excursion, Weeny, not content with the sofa cushions, took to Mother's bed, running right over her face in the middle of the night. This caused quite the upset. Indeed, Anne wrote a couple of hundred words on the back of that disaster.

I have fond memories of laying trails of hamster mix and conducting night-time patrols with a torch, before eventually they would be recaptured, usually after about a week, when they were feral enough to inflict a sharp nip.

At the weekends, the pets currently in residence would be packed into the car and transported to our country cottage, along with Nanny and the suitcases. Goldilocks chose a wheat-field to make good her escape. I had taken her for a 'walk' secure in the knowledge that she was safe in a polythene bag, which I had taken the precaution of putting in my coat pocket. I shall never forget the trauma of putting my hand inside, only to pull out the empty bag complete with a small hole in one corner.

She, too, chose not to return.

We had ducklings for a few weeks in the country. They splashed around in a small concrete pond, and shat as soon as I picked one up. My mother certainly wouldn't have ordered these in. I suspect my father, Macdonald Hastings (who at this point was on the *Tonight* television programme reporting on things of a 'country' nature) was using them to illustrate some point or another – ducks versus chickens, that sort of thing. I cannot remember them as adults – they certainly didn't get to the *à l'orange* stage.

Anne hated cats. In fact she had not a good word to say for them, she felt they were malevolent. But we did have dogs. One mongrel was brought back from the Seychelles by my father, who had decided to cast himself away on a desert island, to write a newspaper story on the 'real Robinson Crusoe'. He was accompanied on this trip by a turtle, Fifi, and the dog, Friday. Friday did rather well on the island, living off small birds and his wits. My father less well. Anyway, he brought Friday back to England. Really, the less said about this sorry tale the better, but Friday, who loved people with a passion, despised anything on four legs. He had spent six months in quarantine, which had not helped his temperament. In the country no sheep were safe, and in Kensington Gardens all other dogs were treated as either mortal enemies or a tasty treat. He was also totally un-house-trained. I, of course, loved Friday. Even Mother liked Friday. But he was unmanageable. Father, thinking he was solving the problem that he had created, had Friday put down.

My mother was absolutely livid, unable to understand why my father had not attempted to find the dog a suitable home – which would really have been back on the island, where he had flourished. Anyway, the combination of the Friday débâcle and his desert island foray was the finale to their relationship, and by 1962 my parents had divorced.

The last pet to enter Anne's life was a miniature long-haired dachshund. My stepfather, Osbert, took it upon himself to give my mother a dog as a surprise gift. I cannot imagine why. He had managed single-handed to locate a breeder (this in itself was a miracle) and went alone to collect it at the railway station (another first). The dog was called Maud, after Osbert's great cartoon creation Maudie Littlehampton. My mother was astonished and appalled, and kept saying to me 'Why on *earth* did you let him do it?', deciding to blame both of us. Osbert was not a bit perturbed and nor was I. Maud was very pretty, and very passive. She fitted well into our lives (by then we had moved into Osbert's digs, a flat on Eaton Square). Maud was cared for primarily by Anne and our cook, Martha. Maud turned out to have a very delicate digestion, and could only survive on the lightest chicken risotto, which Martha would cook in weekly batches. I don't remember Osbert ever taking Maud for a turn around the square, and I was not much better. In her later years Maud would reside in the country, living with Mrs Mansell in a nearby cottage. Anne would collect Maud on Friday night and return her to Mrs Mansell on Monday morning, a system which worked for everyone, including Maud, who, as Mother frequently remarked, was 'surprisingly well adjusted'.

Osbert for a time also kept small finches, in an ornate birdcage, brought back from a holiday in Tunisia. Again, it is probably better not to dwell too long on their short lives, and the cage was eventually passed to me, minus the finches, to use as a decorative *objet* in my room.

Our pets always paid their way. Readers were riveted to learn about the trials and tribulations of pet ownership via Anne's page. Indeed, Anne's piece on budgies, a eulogy to the little bird, was probably responsible for a major boost in sales that week. Slightly ironic, as she was always of the firm belief that birds should be outside on the wing, to be enjoyed in their natural habitat, not behind bars. Indeed, she loved nothing more than watching the robins, blue tits and nuthatches that assembled on my bird table, just a foot from the kitchen window, and could sit for hours entranced at their behaviour. Pets were an area where she indulged the team, always against her better judgement.

25 May 1957

WELL, I NEVER THOUGHT I'D FALL FOR A BUDGIE!

Three months ago we bought a budgerigar. Up till that glorious day I never knew anyone who kept a budgerigar, heard anyone mention a budgerigar, or thought it conceivable that I would ever give a second thought to a budgerigar.

But now I have discovered that the whole world is teeming with budgerigars. Sir Winston Churchill can't travel without one. Sir Malcolm Sargent has his bath with one on his head. *There are more caged birds in this country as pets than cats or dogs.* In the last five years the number has swollen to a cool ten million. With three months' bird experience behind me, I feel qualified to talk a bit about their advantages.

THEY ARE ideal pets for busy people. They take very little time to look after, and don't need grooming, as they do the job themselves. You can leave them alone in the daytime without their pining, so long as you make a fuss of them when you get in.

THEY ARE the answer to living in a flat. No trailing around the streets to give them a run.

THEY ARE easy to transport if you go away. Alternatively, it is always easy to find friends to take them for a day or two, where it may be difficult to park a dog or cat.

THEY ARE cheap to feed.

THEY ARE adored by children, and become very tame within two or three weeks. A child of five can look after one, and older children will want to keep one or two pairs and breed from them.

I have quite lost any scruples I had about keeping birds in cages. Ours flies all over the house, and is very affectionate, and hops back into his cage when he is tired. He sings a lot, and seems happy.

Budgies are born comedians. Ours fell into a cup of tea one day and was so thrilled at the success of his act that he repeats it to boring point.

(P.S. Remind me to tell you sometime of our *ghastly* experience a while back with a tank of tropical fish. In off-colour moments, the smell comes back to me still.)

Osbert with the prized birdcage,
brought back from a holiday in Tunisia.

Anne and Christmas

Christmas was always spent at Anne's cottage on the Berkshire Downs. As can be seen from reading her articles on the subject, Anne did not enjoy the festive season My father and, later, my stepfather could be relied on, if reminded, to open bottles, but did little else; but this wasn't the reason. She just disliked the tinsel, glitter and general cant that surrounded the event. Anne put on a jolly – indeed, from a child's point of view, excellent – pretence. Indulging the paper chains and traditions until she reached a point where she didn't have to, and I took over.

The tree, when I was a very young child, stood at a healthy height, scraping the cottage ceiling, but with each passing year, as I got taller it became smaller. Soon it needed to be placed on a side table to be spotted. Over subsequent years the size reduced a bit more, until it really was more of a branch on top of the bookcase. Eventually she managed to replace the offending object completely with a jug of winter-flowering viburnum cut from the garden, which reminded her of spring, and really cheered her along.

Some years we had huge coloured bulbs draped over the tree, other times we had candles, placed in metal holders that could be clipped at jaunty angles over the branches. (The fact that the tree never caught fire is proof that we were watched over by the angels, as my brother would certainly have considered the amusement value to be gained from angling a candle closer to the needles.)

In later years Osbert, who thought our tree fairy a dismal affair, whittled a shape out of a piece of kindling and stuck paper to the wood prior to drawing on an angelic face and costume in true Lancaster tradition. She resurfaced for quite a few years, daring the flames to engulf her stick body, until small modern fairy lights appeared.

Anne provided my brother and me each with a soft, very long (on account of her leg length) brown cashmere stocking. These dangled outside our bedroom doors on a piece of string. I always had a lemon soap from Bromley's in the toe, which I thought the smartest thing ever. One year I got up to find my stocking was empty. Father Christmas had left a note. Apparently I had asked for too many things, so got nothing. I think this was my brother's idea of a jolly jape, and my mother did have another one filled and ready to go, but nonetheless . . .

The turkey was delivered every Christmas Eve to the back door of the cottage by Mr Shackleton, who bred them up at his farm on the downs. Christmas lunch was traditional and delicious, initially cooked in an ancient Rayburn, before modernity set in and Anne purchased an electric cooker. It was a family affair – although my godfather, Tony Wysard, and his wife, Ruth, who lived locally, often popped by for drinks. I adored Tony, who I never saw at any other time of the year. He always treated me as a grown-up, handing out small bottles of scent and ten-shilling notes.

Mother cooked turkey, year in, year out. She actually kept a count. When she reached the age of sixty-nine, I returned – from a rare outing to the morning church service – to find her raging. As I entered the house, Christmas platitudes were forgotten. 'Where the F-CK have you been?' she cried. 'I've had to lift this 'F-CKING' bird out of the F-CKING oven twice by myself.' (Anne was no stranger to the 'F' word, although it was kept primarily for family consumption.) I knew it had been one turkey too many and from then on she came over to visit us. Disapproving when I added cranberry sauce into the mix ('American import') and beside herself if I made four vegetable dishes ('much too many, dear').

Her pudding of choice came from – yes, you've guessed – Harrods, and always contained a silver sixpence, and there would be a Stilton cheese which was fed with port until it was inedible.

Anne was brilliant at cracker jokes. She could work out the answers to all of them. Maybe, after pulling so many, the answers were locked into her memory, or maybe for a journalist puns and word play are second nature. While the rest of the table were still working out 'Why can't the bike stand up for itself?', Anne, her paper hat askew, would be shouting out, 'Because it's TWO TIRED!' She also enjoyed trivia games, and there was one memorable lunch where the crackers included whistles. We all tooted 'Good King Wenceslas', while Mother pointed the conductor's baton in a threatening way until we had worked up quite a passable rendition.

Anne was not interested in church – rather the reverse – so the season did not hold any religious significance for her. It really was an occasion to be enjoyed for the shortest possible time, quite a scramble to get everything done and dusted – presents opened in the morning, drinks, and lunch served on the dot of 1 o'clock so we could move on with life. The Queen rarely got a look in either – we were probably too busy burning the festive paper, Anne's personal form of a ritual Christmas cleansing.

19 October 1954

BUY ME A USELESS PRESENT – AND MAKE IT A SURPRISE!

LISTEN, SWEETIE I know just how you feel about Christmas: kindly, tolerant and delightfully above it all. You eye me as I shop and cook and wrap things up, with the same indulgent smile you produce when I've spent too much on a hat.

You behave as if Christmas were a harmless plot thought up by me and the children.

You know I find this attitude *slightly* annoying. As I see it, you're in this thing every bit as much as we are. And so I suggest, in the nicest possible way, that you stop being so superior and busy-at-the-office for the next few days and get your teeth into Christmas. Some serious shopping and planning from tomorrow, plus a little *real* help on the day itself will make Christmas twice as much fun for all of us.

LISTEN, SWEETIE About presents . . . as you know, I've practically done the whole job already. I've done the family, and your mother, and your secretary, and that rather frightful girl who so fortunately went to live in New York.

All you've got to do is buy something for *me*. As you seem a bit slow at reading into my mind, might I drop you a hint or two?

I implore you not to buy me anything useful. I'd adore a washing machine or an electric heater at any other time, but not, somehow, at Christmas.

I'd like something frightfully pretty, absolutely useless and a genuine surprise.

I'd be pleased with a bottle of perfume. A piece of antique china or a bowl of hyacinths in bulb, or a fabulously expensive illustrated book. I'd like one of those lunatic little head cushions covered in white organdie, or some actressy underwear, or a pair of bunny-scuff slippers, or a credit at a hat shop or beauty salon.

I'd prefer this to a cheque, which would only go to pay the household bills.

DON'T – this may surprise you – pay twice as much as we can afford. It would worry me stiff.

But DO – wrap it up in some nice Christmassy paper you have bought yourself.

LISTEN, SWEETIE About the commissariat . . . I do think the drinks and cigarettes are down to you. All right; I know you got them last year. But I got very agitated while you chased around at midnight on Christmas Eve trying to buy gin. I'd rather have got it myself. I should love to think it would be in the house by Wednesday.

LISTEN, SWEETIE About Christmas Eve . . . Do try and get home early (*must* the office party go on so long? I'd have thought you saw enough of each other all day without wanting to clink glasses for five hours in the evening). With the decorating, the stockings, the advance cooking, there's more to do on Christmas Eve than on Christmas Day. (And remember to have some spare fairy light bulbs, because if one blows the whole circuit goes phut.)

LISTEN, SWEETIE About Christmas Day itself . . . the biggest thing you could do for me would be to take the kids out for a couple of hours in the morning. But, for heaven's sake, bring them back, bring them back well before one o'clock. (Remember the time you *went out* at one and *got back* at three? Where you got to I never discovered.) And keep the fire up. If there's one thing that makes me lose my angelic temper, it is to wash up and then come in with the coffee to find you snoozing by a dying spark.

It does sound rather a lot doesn't it? And I don't suppose you'll be feeling so tolerant and amused any more. You'll think I've put the cares of the world on your shoulders. But at least you won't have to worry about the Christmas cards, the stockings, the friends abroad, the catering, the tree, the decorations, the wrapping paper, the fancy labels or the crackers.

Because I've done them all already.

WHY DON'T THE RELATIVES LEAVE US ALONE?

Are you going to spend Christmas the way you want to? In the place you like best? With the people of your choice?

I bet you aren't.

Christmas will be ruined for you, this year as every year, by your relatives.

Although we have lived for centuries in families – not in tribes – at Christmas, for no clear reason, relatives who never do a thing for you the rest of the year will invoke the tribal spirit.

Every blood-relation who doesn't know what to do with himself, every connection-by-marriage who is short of interests and friends, will thankfully claim his right to join the clan. And it won't be the merry, likeable relatives who will be coming along. They have made plans of their own.

PARASITES

This is the gift season for parasites. It is the time when the people with empty lives batten on the people with full ones.

Parents will descend on you for the day or for the whole weekend, so that, instead of getting a peaceful break at Christmas, you find yourself running a small but good hotel.

And having to be polite for days on end – that's what kills . . .

Or your in-laws will insist on your abandoning your

own home and going to them. '*You* come to *us*,' they say. 'It will save you all the cooking.'

SELFISH

Actuated by diabolical selfishness, all of them.

The in-laws aren't the slightest bit interested in saving you the trouble. They know in their hearts that you want to be in your own home. But they have an octopus-like determination to get their tentacles round you.

WRONG AGE

The odd thing is that, however old you are, you never seem to be in the right age group to call the tune. And you haven't chosen your own pattern for Christmas Day since you were ten.

In your teens you longed for a young people's party on Christmas Day, but it had to be relatives, most of them very old.

Newly married, you wanted to spend Christmas together, but you were winkled out to join your parents, grandparents, and a sprinkling of cousins and aunts.

With a young family, you thought you were safe and could stay in your own home. So you did – but a bunch of relatives came to you, and had the nerve to complain at the way your children behaved.

WE PLANNED

Will I, at sixty, I wonder, be able to plan my own Christmas Day at last? Or will I in my turn be blackmailing my children to amuse me?

P.S. This year we made plans. How is it working out?

I S-H-A-L-L B-E I-N T-H-E O-F-F-I-C-E. W-O-R-K-I-N-G. A-L-L C-H-R-I-S-T-M-A-S D-A-Y.

NO, I DON'T WANT A DUSTBIN FOR CHRISTMAS

Unless, of course, you fill it up with jewels

So many competent people give advice on Christmas shopping that I usually lay off the subject.

You don't need me to tell you that a teddy bear is a teddy bear or that barbola book ends are available if wanted.

But this year I have seen such really nauseating gift suggestions that I feel like weighing in with a little guidance. Any manufacturer who makes any end product is shooting it out in gift packaging.

What would you say if someone you trusted gave you a box of barrier cream? (*My comment would be unsuitable for publication in a family newspaper.*)

How would you feel if someone threw their arms round you and said 'For you, my love,' and shyly handed you a holly-covered box of deodorants?

There are many necessities of life which it is best to buy for oneself. I don't want my friends, when they think of me, to go rootling through the ironmonger's and the chemist's.

Yet this week I have seen the following displayed as gifts in magazines, catalogues, and shop windows: medicated skin soap, non-greasy hair cream, youthify skin food, plastic food bags, hairnets, string bags, corsets, dustbins, flannels, loofahs, sieves.

No, friends, when you think of me connect my name with the jeweller's. Or, if this is for any reason impracticable, then make for the bookshop, the flower shop, the sweet shop, the decorator's or the fashion store.

Christmas presents, however useful, and however cheap, should have the blessed virtue of charm.

9 December 1956

CRACKERS – BETTER COUPLETS

At a children's tea party there was the usual disappointment over the crackers. Some were cased in such thick paper that even the fathers couldn't pull them. (*How can any manufacturer make such an idiotic mistake?*)

Some had negligible contents.

Later, at home, I took out three of the crackers I have bought for Christmas and sampled them.

One contained a motto and a circle of crepe paper.

One contained a motto and a whistle that wouldn't blow.

One contained a motto, a cap and a firework snake. This was the only one which could conceivably be considered a good tenpennyworth.

If high costs and purchase tax make better value impossible then I suggest that cracker-makers put ten good ones in a box instead of a dozen poor ones.

And surely it wouldn't cost much to improve the mottoes?

One of my sample three read: 'Why is a watch like a river?' 'Because it doesn't run long without winding.' Who is going to get a laugh out of that?

Why not some couplets by John Betjeman? Some Christmas *pensées* by Cyril Connolly?

Or tiny cartoons by Langdon, Lancaster, Anton, Sprod?

That (in cracker language) should provide plenty of Yuletide mirth.

NOTES

John Betjeman (1906-1984) Poet. Lover of a good cracker joke.

Cyril Connolly (1903-1974) Literary critic and writer.

Charles Landon (1878-1937) American cartoonist and teacher.

Anton (Antonia Yeoman, 1907-1970) Her cartoons appeared in *Punch*, *Lilliput*, *The New Yorker*.

George Sprod (1919-2003) Australian cartoonist. He contributed to *Punch* magazine during the 1950s.

Propping up the bar for this iconic
shot for Picture Post, 1941.

Anne and Education

'We are still waiting for the penny to drop,' was the damning sentence handed down by the headmistress at my first and only school, Francis Holland, Sloane Square. So was my mother. In fact so was I. It had been thought that I would spend my early years at F.H before moving seamlessly to my mother's alma mater, St Paul's. However, It became increasingly clear that I was never going to hack it as a Paulina, so it was simpler for me to remain at F.H. Anne found my lack of academic prowess surprising. She herself had been a naturally gifted child, in fact she was always placed in a class with an older age group, as it was generally felt she needed to be 'stretched'. My brother too was academically gifted, exams a treat rather than the horror they were to me. Having said that, I loved the companionship provided by school. If only it had been an entirely social event with the unpleasant incomprehensible bits eliminated, it really would have been bliss.

As a family we are not university material. I, obviously, never went, but my mother, my brother, and my own daughter all left before completing their degrees. They were driven by the desire to work. The social angle which is always mentioned as one of the main joys of a university life was no compensation. They had all had enough of formal education.

Anne went to Somerville College, Oxford, on a classical scholarship. For five terms she consumed Greek and Latin, languages and literature, but while she loved the work she found Oxford a gloomy place. She described the spires as 'rain-washed', with tolling bells, and complained about miasmas rising from the rivers. Making it sound more like a town from a *Hammer* film than an idyll in the home counties. She had expected brilliant conversation, and the freedom that was lacking at home. Instead, she found the male undergraduates treated women with suspicion, and Somerville closed the gates every night at 10.30, making it more like boarding school than a place of enlightenment. Higher education was still unusual for women and the college had yet to find its stride.

For all that Anne managed to fall madly in love and was proposed to three times during her two-year sojourn, which by any standards is quite good going, so it can't have been a total washout.

She left in June 1933, to the fury of her father, but not until she had obtained a First in Honour Moderations (Mods).

Anne was desperate for that First, as men and women took the exam on equal terms, and here was proof that women were *not* an inferior sex, an idea that was apparently still rife at Oxford.

Anne certainly did not believe that university was for the masses. Some people benefited, others did not, and to expect that everyone should automatically go on to higher education was simply not common sense.

Nor did she think that a university education should be a direct route to job security. A university was not a training college. Anne was a firm believer in study for study's sake. She was also very against students paying for their courses. The idea of a young person starting out in life with a large debt really upset her. She was a great advocate for free tuition, and thought a healthy society should invest in education.

Luckily, she was not alive to learn about 'no platforming' or 'safe space'. She would have been incandescent to hear that students were not up to the task of debate. Everyone should have a voice, and the audience should be prepared to robustly challenge the view presented.

'No platform', however offensive the students found the speaker, was an idea she would simply have considered moronic. I can hear her now: 'What are they there *for*?'

I am not sure she would have been very keen on the 'me too' movement, either. Anne abhorred violence against women, and bullying was given short shrift, but as one of the first women to compete on a level with the opposite sex, she had speedily learnt how to put down an unwelcome advance with a few withering words. She also thought the best place to meet men was the workplace.

Anne thought an education in the classics would always see you employed. In her case it proved true. Obviously, she made her living as a writer. In addition, for thirteen years Mother was on the panel of the radio show *My Word!* She had taken over from the journalist Nancy Spain, who had, shockingly, died in an aircraft crash on her way to Aintree racecourse for the Grand National. The year was 1964, and Anne, as Nancy's replacement, was to partner Denis Norden. On the opposite team sat Frank Muir and his partner, the film critic Dilys Powell. Anne loved the show, and she loved her fellow panellists. She called it 'a stroke of luck, rare in professional life, to work with such clever and friendly people'. I loved the show too. As a teenager too young to be left on my own I would tag along with Mother. Everyone met up in the Sherlock Holmes pub for a drink and a chat and I would be greeted as one of the team. We then walked around the corner to the theatre, where a studio audience was waiting, and

I took my place to enjoy the show. Frank would always give me a wave and a wink before the start. He really was the kindest of men. I won't forget the opening words in a hurry: '*My Word!* is a word game, played by people whose business is words . . .' Both Anne and Dilys used their knowledge of the classics to work out the origins and derivations of words. Frank and Denis were of course the stars and really just brilliant, their ad libbing an inspiration. Their set story piece for the last round of every show gained a cult following. I think it is the only time that Anne got the billing 'performer'. She also enjoyed the celebrity that *My Word!* brought. It was broadcast all over the world. Anne, as far as I know, was never asked to appear on television, but she relished radio, and missed it when, in 1979, because of Osbert's increasing ill health, she decided she had to leave the show.

Anne never really discussed, or tried to address, my academic failure. She just left it at that. I muddled along and left at the earliest opportunity. It must have been a blow to her, as intellect in our household was a much-valued commodity. The word 'clever' was high praise, 'intelligent conversation' the Holy Grail. Like a lot of school dunces, I had learnt to deflect my inadequacies by making people laugh, and I made Mother laugh. Not with jolly jokes, but with irony. We shared a sense of humour. I did not join the old girls' society, Mother deciding she had paid quite enough for my lack of education, and the small fee required for me to join was her Bridge Too Far.

31 March 1957

CURTAIN UP

This week I went to a prep school play. A completely successful occasion, because the play was specially written for the boys of twelve or thirteen who were to act in it.

It was a Tudor adventure story, well within their grasp.

Some blood-and-guts, a loud explosion, and a Spanish plot against King Hal aroused the gusto of both cast and audience.

But it's surprising how many schools choose unsuitable, even embarrassing, plays for children. *The School for Scandal*, a comedy demanding the highest style and polish, is a frequent unhappy choice. So is *The Importance of Being Earnest*, unactable below the Gielgud–Edith Evans level.

So are the weightier plays of Shakespeare.

I shall never believe that Lady Macbeth ('I have given suck and know/ How tender 'tis to love the babe that milks me') is a suitable role for a girl of twelve. (*I made my debut in the part.*)

Or that Richard II ('Hath sorrow struck/So many blows upon this face of mine/And made no deeper wounds') is within the comprehension of a happy little tadpole of eleven.

I asked John Fernald, President of RADA, what plays he would recommend for children.

'**NOT** mannered comedy and **NOT** Shakespeare. The children must of course understand what they are saying. The best plays I know are those of Nicholas Stuart Grey, who has dramatized the Grimm and Hans Andersen stories in a style which is simple and unwhimsy.'

Schools with a leaning for Sheridan and Congreve, kindly note.

TRICKY

I have been reading the exam questions of a girl of nine. Describe in not more than eight lines:

a) The coming of Christianity to Britain.
b) The reasons for the decline of the Roman Empire.
c) The Italian Renaissance.

Well – could you do it?

NOTES

John Fernald (1905–1985) Theatre director, Principal of the Royal Academy of Dramatic Art 1955–1966)

Nicholas Stuart Grey (1922–1981) Actor and playwright, best known for his work in children's theatre.

13 October 1957

WHO WOULD YOU LIKE FOR YOUR MOTHER – DR EDITH OR ME?

Every Sunday I chew my pencil and scratch out a letter to my son. Every mother with a child away at school, at work, or on National Service does much the same thing. My letter is just a string of family gossip. All the news and small details which keep him in touch. But on reading Edith Summerskill's *Letters to my Daughter*, published this week, I'm wondering if I'm off beam. Each of her letters is a self-contained political tract.

Which of us is right ? Am I too trivial? Or is she too inhuman? I'd like your honest views. Below I print off a typical letter of my sort and imaginary letter to the same boy in the style of Dr E:

Darling M –

I'm miserable that you've got a cold, but I'm afraid we've all got them. I've sent you one of those model planes to construct to help pass the time. I hope it's complicated enough – there are 157 different parts.

Don't collapse, but yesterday Chirpy nearly met a martyr's death. I shan't let him out at mealtimes again. We had some boling hot onion soup, and he flew straight at my soup plate and fell half in before I grabbed him.

There was soup all over the table, great alarm, and he had to be washed. He seems in good fettle now, but smells strongly of onions.

I am making sensational plans for the Christmas holidays, I think we have all rather *had* the circus, and I thought we might break new ground and go to an ice show. What do you think?

Have sent you some grub as requested, and a revolting-looking chocolate cake with pink decorations. I must say your taste in food is very immature.

Have you run out of things to read? I can't find any more war books – you've read them all. But I hear there is a new series coming out called *Great Disasters of the World*, which sounds just your meat.

Clare loved your birthday present – I think it was her favourite – and the party went off with a bang. I must say when I think of the horrors of the parties when you were young – all those ghastly little boys fighting and smashing things – a little girls' party seems very sedate. I can't tell you how sweet they all looked in their party frocks. One actually wore face powder!

I am repainting your desk in a tasteful emerald green, and it looks terrific. You also badly need a new rug. Would you like one for Christmas? No I was afraid not.

Daddy has zoomed off to Scotland on some mad enterprise. He sent his love.

Where are you in form? If you could get one place higher this term, we'd be thrilled.

Pots of love from us all,

Mummy

Darling M –

Now that you are eleven, I think it is time for you to give serious consideration to the problem of the emancipation of women.

Happily, in this country, great strides have been taken in the past twenty-five years towards true equality of the sexes. Political equality is only partially achieved, and we must fight on until the rate for the job is universal.

But the hardest struggle is still ahead in the realm of social equality. In too many homes today it is assumed that the husband can earn the family income, while the wife remains chained to the sink.

Until it is customary for the husband and wife to divide the work according to their aptitudes, there will be millions of unhappy and frustrated families, and much of the finest resources of the nation will be sadly squandered.

Think these problems over while you are standing idle playing goalie in the football field.

I am a little puzzled by your request for additional nutriment. I understand that the calorie intake allowed by the school catering section is adequate for health and I doubt it is wise to acquire a taste for extra luxury foods which it may not always be possible or advisable to gratify.

Yesterday I went to Little Mudford in Staffordshire, as a member of a delegation to a conference on te Nationalization of Housing.

Through a gross piece of inefficiency on the part of the reception committee, there was nobody there to meet us. Imagine a group of two Privy Councillors and the Woman's Page Editor of the *Sunday Express* standing in rain at a wayside station without transport.

When all property is nationalized, these annoying incidents will no longer occur.

On Tuesday, I attended a luncheon party in Westminster at which I sat next to Mr Tom Driberg.

I had an intensely interesting conversation with Mr Driberg on the subject of automation in China.

I hope you have thought over my comments last week about racial discrimination, and have spoken to your headmaster about eliminating boxing from the school curriculum.

Fond love,

Mama

CHOOSE YOUR MOTHER FOR £5

Who would you rather have for a mother – Dr Summerskill or me? Write your answer and reason on a postcard and send it to the *Sunday*

Express by Thursday 17 Oct. £5 for the best postcard.

To win the prize you don't have to choose me. Final selection will be by the Editor, who says he'd much prefer Dr Summerskill.

THE ANSWERS
ME OR DR EDITH?
'I WOULD HATE YOU BOTH'

Me for mother, or Dr Summerskill? The competition I set last week brought in thousands of fiery postcards from both adults and children.

Many readers say that, faced with such a frightful choice, they would opt for being orphans.

Setting aside the jokes about margarine, Norwegian ancestry and funny hats, and the interesting entry signed Wolfenden Minor, some meaty points came out about the relationship between mothers and children.

'I'd choose you, because an absent child wants to hear everything that happens at home, however small. If the thread of affection is broken, it's never mended again.'

'Dr Summerskill, because she remains a mother and doesn't want to be an elder sister. I hate your matey style.'

'I know you'd disgrace me on speech day. You'd snuffle into a hanky.'

'I'd choose you because you include a message from your husband. I've read Dr Summerskill's letter from end to end, and her husband isn't mentioned once.'

'Dr S., because children always swing away from their parents. Sons of clergymen become actors, and so on.'

'Our responsibility to our children is to love and trust and enjoy them. Let the schools do the educating.'

'I'd hate you both, because you publish your letters.' (This hit a bullseye.)

Children who send postcards are divided on the subject of fashion. Some yearn for a well-dressed mother to make a splash on school occasions. Some prefer a mother to sink into the background.

But they are all united on the subject of food. A mother's first duty is to fill the cake tin.

Nobody raised one point which I think is important. I believe that your children have an influence on you, as well as you on them. Family ideas are a two-way traffic.

I was criticized for using slang expressions to curry favour with the young. But in fact, I've picked up the expressions from my children, and am quite likely to say 'Crikey' at a business meeting. In the same way, because my daughter likes red curtains, I find I like them too.

NOTE
Dr Edith Summerskill (1919– 2003) Physician, ardent feminist, Labour politician and writer.

A drawing by Osbert of me in Rome, 1966.
I was fifteen, the dress and bag are by Biba,
and the doll accessory was very on-trend.

Anne and Teenagers

Anne found work much more alluring than small children, so, although I was very well cared for, it was mostly by others. I cannot recall her engaging much in day-to-day life. School holidays when I was tiny would be spent with Nanny in Frinton, which Nanny adored and Mother considered an offshoot of hell, so she would drop us off and beat a hasty retreat back to London. This was not a sadness. Nanny and I loved Frinton.

My parents divorced in 1961, and my father married the publisher Anthea Joseph in 1962. My brother elected to live with them in the country. Nanny by this time had retired and I was overseen by a succession of cheery Spanish au pairs. It was all change for Anne too. She had 'crossed the street' and was now working for the *Daily Mail*, sharing an office with Bernard Levin, and she seemed busier than ever. She also seemed to be permanently cross, a state which lasted for about two years. Work, divorce, and dealing with home, had left her stressed and unhappy.

When I turned thirteen, there was a definite change in Anne's personality. At the time, with youthful preoccupation, I simply imagined that with my increasing age I had developed a more interesting edge. Then, of course, I realized that the change had nothing at all to do with me, an outside force had come into our lives. Anne had fallen in love. Now she was simply *happy*.

I was fifteen when Anne actually married Osbert, but he had become a part of our lives a good bit earlier. His arrival was, from all points of view, an entirely positive event.

Osbert did not like conflict, which is perhaps what made him the ideal stepfather. He had absolutely no desire to boss me around, tell me off or mould me, he accepted that where my mother lived so did I, and we became from day one best friends and allies.

Osbert didn't call me 'Clare' very often. I was 'dear child' or – his nickname for me – 'Trendy'. John Betjeman once confided that for years he had assumed Trendy was my given name.

After their marriage we moved from a huge rented flat overlooking the Cromwell Road into Osbert's flat in Eaton Square. Although this was clearly a step up in terms of location, it had not been designed with me in mind. Apart from a massive and gloriously theatrical drawing room, the flat consisted of small rooms leading off a winding staircase. My bedroom was at the top and was just that – a room for my bed.

Misery! Osbert and John don't get on.

But all was not lost. The lease included a tiny basement room, hidden away among the hot water boilers several houses down. I think it was originally supposed to be of use for a live-in maid, but it was converted to become my 'pad' and I had my own key to my own house in Eaton Square. Apart from running the gamut of a terrifying and leering porter, this was to be a room of my own. It was also the home for various waifs and strays, that was obligatory in the sixties. My little room was much in demand. There was always someone looking for temporary accommodation and a spot to doss. Although the room was a good block down from the main house, I was always in fear that Mother would be rounding the corner and bump into one or other of my 'tenants' emerging. By any stretch of the imagination they looked unlikely to be residents of the usual Eaton Square persuasion.

It didn't take me very long to work out that Osbert was 'cool'. His friends were 'cool', his car was 'cool' (a black mini with a plastic wicker finish), even his drawing was 'cool'. My only 'A', in geography, was the result of his help with my homework. I was having difficulty drawing a map of Canada, and O cheered it up no end with the addition of mooses and mounties. But 'cool' Osbert really came to the fore in 1964 when he was asked to chair a Foyle's Literary Lunch at the Dorchester. The lunch was in honour of a new book, *In His Own Write*, by John Lennon. I was beside myself. Mother and I were also invited, not to the main table, but to one with a good view of the action, so I was able to gaze on Osbert eating lunch slap next door to a Beatle. I was convinced John would be added to the inner circle. I was planning our life together. Not to be. Despite being told by John that he had a 'lucky face', Osbert completely let me down by finding my hero the reverse of alluring.

Osbert and I also went together to see the musical *Hair*, without Anne, who did not fancy the outing. I do remember teenage embarrassment, cringing in my seat as the stage filled up with nakedness. Osbert, for whom nudity held no fear, was completely unfazed and professed to have enjoyed the evening.

As the mother of a teenager, Anne really came into her own. Her own upbringing had been one of rules and regulations, Anne never got on with her own parents and so was determined to be easy-going. I was allowed to go on marches (everyone went on marches), walk barefoot through London (everyone walked barefoot through London), and stay on my own in the flat while they disappeared for weekends to the cottage (now this *was* unusual, nobody I knew had a posh home to call their own from Friday lunch to Monday morning). Anne had accounts at all the local shops, and I learnt to cook during those weekends, running an upmarket soup kitchen from the flat. Everything to be returned to a pristine condition for their return, so they were none the wiser for the intrusions. I had no concept of food seasons, so raspberries in December and asparagus in January were standard on the menu. The butcher, baker and candlestick-maker all cheered as I approached, but at home no one ever commented on my food consumption, except that Mother did once mention that the milk bill had drastically reduced when I left home (the joints of spring lamb having, apparently, passed her by).

Anne was a generous provider of mini-skirts and catsuits from Biba, Bus Stop and Countdown. I remember my first foray into Biba in Abingdon Road – I bought a divine mini-dress complete with matching handbag and a green wood bead bracelet. Op Art berets, plastic raincoats, PVC trouser suits – I owned the lot, and I felt I needed them. I was a gawky teen, with terrible teeth, and my best friend looked like Françoise Hardy and brought traffic to a standstill. Satin flares and a crop top really were a necessity if I was to attempt to hold my own. The King's Road was only a five-minute walk away, and you needed to be at the top of your game to create any sort of impression.

Anne was also very relaxed about boyfriends. She never asked me anything about my relationships, nor did she discuss any basic health issues. When I first experienced a period, I really did think I was bleeding out. Mother very calmly produced a fat packet of towels and a hideous belt, and passed them over with no word of 'how to' or any sort of explanation, just said, 'Oh, I was expecting this', and left me to work out the practicalities. We certainly never sat down for the talk about sex and pregnancy, but then I am not sure you did in the sixties. I think the problem page of *Jackie* magazine was everyone's bible of choice for information of a sexual nature and, as Mother had it delivered weekly into the house alongside the dailies, she probably thought she had that base covered.

I left home in my late teens, really by accident rather than design. I was experiencing first love, and had taken to staying over a couple of nights a week. Anne casually asked one evening if I was thinking of leaving home. Up to that point I had not given the matter even a moment's thought. I said, 'Yes.' Anne said, 'When?' I said, 'Tomorrow.'

So tomorrow I hailed a taxi, filled it with a couple of suitcases along with Osbert's ornamental birdcage and repaired to a house in Balham. This would not have been Anne's location of choice, as at this point Balham had yet to dip so much as a small toe into the waters of gentrification.

She came to visit a week later. As I put her back on the train to Victoria, there were tears in her eyes – but she never said, 'Don't.'

Anne and Travel

Of course Anne loved to travel, and she was paid to travel, writing articles from countries across the world. Rome and France were regular stop-offs for the collections, as was New York. Later she went further afield, to Japan, Africa, and Russia, catching planes, and crossing time zones at a time when it was still exhilarating just to visit Heathrow. The golden age of plane travel. It was also an excellent method of avoiding my father. One came home and the other one left. Often, they both left.

In 1960 we went to the South of France on holiday. I was nine. Earlier that year Mother and I had been photographed for *The People* newspaper. We were posed by the cottage gate and at the request of the photographer lifted our arms in a wave, while attempting to look poignant and sad as my father walked off down the road into the middle distance. He stopped and turned slightly at the last moment to look over his shoulder and wave a 'goodbye' to his family (my mother and me – my brother being away at school). I did not know at the time that he had been paid by the *The People* to cast himself away on an uninhabited island in the Seychelles, to live as a modern-day Robinson Crusoe, accompanied only by Fifi, a giant tortoise, and Friday the dog. He was unfit, in his fifties, and lived largely on a diet of cigarettes and pink gin. I was often brought in as the token child for a photo shoot, so I didn't think twice about the ramifications of this particular one.

Anne met up with Mac twice during this folly – soon after his departure and again on his return. Initially their paths crossed in Nairobi. By some extraordinary quirk of fate, Mother and Mac, unknown to either of them, were both lodging at the New Stanley Hotel. She was off on an assignment for the *Mail* and due to fly into the Masai Mara, while Father was en route for the Seychelles to locate his desert island. Thereafter, for thirty-six excoriating days, he immersed himself in the Seychelles project, which led to his near-death, and was to be the defining nail in the coffin of their marriage. He was returned to London by stretcher after barely surviving. Mother had run out of sympathy for Mac's shenanigans. Our holiday to Cavalière had been planned for some time, and off we went as soon as he came home. Father was left to arrange his souvenirs of conch shells and stingray tails from the bed. As far as I recall he was no longer in residence on our return. I still have one of the shells.

Anne travelled a lot for her work, but it was a road trip with friends to Czechoslovakia in her early twenties that kick-started her fascination with travel. You might think that she ran from plane to plane with aplomb, but she was a nervous traveller. Not in the sense that she thought she might fall from the sky, but she became anxious, first about leaving home, and then about the travel arrangements themselves. This would translate into a certain edginess. Anne certainly covered all bases. With Anne in charge you could just sit back and enjoy the ride. On one trip to Italy with Osbert, Mother had every official in Rome airport combing the skies for my missing suitcase. O and I lurked behind a pillar, and just listened on in awe. We preferred to cheer from a distance, which Mother had noticed, not best pleased at our lack of support. We agreed it simpler just to let her get on with it.

Mother was happiest on her travels in Greece with Osbert. Wherever we journeyed Osbert found friends. Up a mountain top, 'Dear boy, how are you?'; on a deserted beach, 'Oh I say! Let's have a snifter.' He seemed to have a knack of locating company. I was a teenager on these outings, only longing to acquire a suntan, and having little truck with the endless round of Byzantine churches they both seemed drawn to. The churches were always locked, the priest with the key probably off visiting friends in the next-door village. After a couple of churches I would wait in the car, hoping this would foreshorten their visits. Seen one . . .

Osbert and Mother certainly did not crave a boutique hotel. Some of the places we visited were very primitive. Greece had yet to be discovered by the package tour companies. We stayed at one village in Crete where I was horrified to find that our running water was the village well, and the lavatory a plank with a hole in the ground, and a bucket of lime, which I found challenging. Mother, Osbert and I shared a room, each on a wire mesh bed with a filthy mattress and a pillow filled with rocks. They adored it. The painter John Craxton had found it for them and was a constant visitor, while staying in the next-door cottage were Stephen Spender's son Matthew and his wife, Maro. They took it upon themselves to entertain me, and I would nip in to visit them every day. This was also the only time that Mother ever censored my literature. They had lent me *Fanny Hill* to read, which I was much enjoying, and kept by my bed. Day three it vanished. I didn't enquire as to the book's whereabouts, I had read enough to realize that Anne had decided to return it to source. Matthew also lost his glasses down the well while bringing up a bucket of water. He climbed down and got them back. How exactly I don't recall, they must have got lodged on some brickwork, but I remember the village gathered round and cheered.

Anne coming down the steps of a
BOAC plane, in the early 1950s.

Anne - age cannot wither her, nor custom stale . . .

Of course, wherever they went Osbert carried his green-cloth-backed sketchbooks. Drawing scenes, people and churches as the mood took him. Often people would collect just to watch him. He never minded, and Mother would sit contentedly watching him too. These were some of the happiest times in her life. They also shared a fondness for a picnic, Osbert enchanted by the concept of the paper napkin.

After Osbert died Mother didn't feel like going anywhere. Then a couple of years later, after we had been out for a chopstick lunch, Anne went off piste and booked a trip to Malaysia for her, me, and my daughter, Calypso, then aged nine. It was to be an adventure, somewhere she would never have travelled to with Osbert. I was in slight trepidation about the outing, but once there was determined that we should all have a good time. As the designated driver and map-reader I was in charge of day-to-day activities. Anne was quickly bored by a beach, so I packed the team into the car, off on an outing to a lake recommended by the guide book for the beauty of its water lilies. Instead of the planned route, I took a wrong turn and ended going down a dirt track to arrive by the shore of a huge river. There, loitering at the water's edge, was a villager, on his own, passing the time of day. He smiled and waved, pointing with enthusiasm to his shallow dugout canoe. We all got in, as if it were a trip up the Thames at Sonning. Off we paddled across the expanse of water, before hanging a left into jungle. Every now and again I got out and helped to push the canoe along increasingly shallow water, into denser and denser foliage. Mother sat calmly and keenly with Calypso, taking in the huge tree roots and the beauty of the creepers. We kept going for about an hour. It passed my mind several times that we had probably been kidnapped, and, if so, would my brother cheer or spring into action to sort out the ransom? I was in a sort of silent despair when suddenly the trees opened out and we sallied forth out on to the lake, which was awash with the promised flowers. The boatman leant down and pulled out two huge lily leaves, which he fashioned into hats for Anne and Calypso.

Hooray, result. Anne wore the hat for the rest of the day. She was never remotely phased by anything of an unusual nature, as long as she thought things were going to plan. I, of course, was left palpitating.

On the same holiday, I mislaid Calypso in a multi-storey hotel in Kuala Lumpur, to find her some hours later learning to create ice sculpture in the kitchens. This was quite tiring as I had to navigate a lot of lifts and many corridors to prevent Anne discovering my mishap. The key to holiday harmony was not to over-share.

12 December 1954

AMERICA – ALWAYS SOMETHING NEW TO SEE

Ideas, ideas, they pour out of Americans. Every day, every hour, you see something new.

I SAW many more painted walls than wallpaper, the colours bright and clear. Most successful: persimmon red walls in a nursery with lots of white woodwork.

I SAW the new Gourielli Men's Shop, a men's boutique-cum-beauty-salon, where a man can get such treats as a printed gingham tie or a manicure.

I SAW escalators instead of lifts in the newest offices.

I SAW motor cars with the new, big, curved windscreens that give wonderful vision.

I SAW transparent muslins through which the sunlight poured unchecked. They hang straight, are not crossed over or draped. But they are scalloped and embroidered, seem all airiness and light.

I SAW black linen tablecloths bordered in black lace. What a setting for china!

But, oh, it was good to get back to our sense of fairness. When a woman in a London shop said, 'You were before me, I think,' I nearly fainted.

THIS IS PARIS

It's not like me to count my blessings, But I must say I'm quite glad I *don't* live in Paris. It's not all flower markets and wine by the carafe.

The way the shops shut up for August makes house-keeping a nightmare for the few left behind – and even in Paris *somebody* must work in August, or France wouldn't merely run down, I suppose it would stop.

Parisians talk of nothing else now but the cost of living. Prices are soaring. Even wine is going up, for the fifth time this year.

The French haven't the faintest idea of comfort. Tapestries, hard gilt chairs and bibelots are no substitute for the deep sofas, good beds and hospitable fireplaces of the English home.

In Paris, even the grandest house is basically bleak.

TRAVEL WITHOUT TEARS

If there's one time above all others when I love my children, it's when we travel.

Then their thoughtfulness, their peacefulness, their ability to go without food and to endure petty discomforts without complaint reach their greatest heights.

Let's be honest, even the shortest journey with a child is unmitigated torture. But if you want to come out alive:

- **Take** enormous supplies of good, plain water. A thirsty child is going to be cross.
- **Take** something to wash with. A child with dried chocolate on its face is more than flesh and blood can bear.
- **Dress** the child coolly. Most journeys are not too chilly, but far too hot.
- **Take** non-starchy food. Say, scotch eggs and lettuce rather than stodgy sandwiches.
- **Don't** let children read in the car. It's an instant way of getting sick.
- **Play** spotting games as long as you can stand them. Points scored for pubs, churches, fat policemen.
- **Stop** frequently on car trips. Five minutes fresh air by the wayside can save hours of disaster. If your husband is the sort who won't stop, drive yourself.

16 January 1955

OH, THE SURPRISES WHEN YOU TRAVEL

A month ago I was in America, meeting pretty girls, talking to big-shot men, eating expensive food, goggling at overflowing shops . . . taking stock of the products of great material wealth and a high standard of living.

A week ago I was in Tunisia, wondering at the unspeakable squalor, squirming free from begging children, sniffing through gorgeous but smelly markets, shying off luscious sweets and fruits because they were covered in flies. Signs of dirt and a low standard of life.

I wonder why the Arabs looked so much happier than the Americans?

If I had to live in a crowded fetid Kairouan, city of two hundred mosques in the centre of an arid plain, or in some small town in Texas or Arizona, I'd go for Kairouan every time.

JUST WONDERFUL

How little one uses one's sense of smell in England. The extraordinary scents of North Africa demand a keener-than-English nose. I don't mean the rancid smells of the back alleys. I mean the wonderful smells of flowers and spices and herbs that sidle along with every breeze. The narcissi are out now. Giant hedges of rosemary border the gardens. And eucalyptus wood is burned in every fire.

TIP FOR TRAVELLERS

If they tell you the plane is full, don't accept it. I got stuck in a fog, took a night train to Paris, was told by officials that there was no hope of a plane from Paris to London for two days. Other travellers were in the same mess. We eyed each other malevolently, wondering who was going to get away first. Well, I did.

Struck lucky

Paris unluckily has two airports. But by chasing from one to the other, trying to gatecrash every plane, I struck lucky on the third go. Some of the passengers, I firmly believe, are waiting in Paris still.

The trouble is you have to ring every airline separately for information, and at 6.30 a.m. you are apt to get no reply.

Couldn't there be some central office, open day and night, with last-minute information about all planes?

24 April 1955

GIVE ME A DREAM ISLAND

THE JOKE
Grim and noisy

At Syracuse I went to see the vast echoing cave known as Dionysius's Ear. The tyrant Dionysius is said to have had it built for a political prison in the fourth century BC, in the shape of an ear. According to the legend, every word spoken by his prisoners was overheard by his spies.

An infinitely tedious guide was demonstrating its echoing power. The cave will catch the faintest rustle.

The guide sang a snatch of an opera. We had to listen to the echo.

He recited a long, unintelligible poem. We had to listen to the echo.

He tore up pieces of paper. We had to listen to the echo. He tore up piece after piece: nothing would stop him. The whole party was bored to death listening to the echo of tearing paper.

Then a Sicilian in the party grinned at the two 50-lire notes he had ready for a tip and tore them in half. He listened with satisfaction to the echo and handed the pieces to the guide.

THE GREENNESS
Almonds and olives

I shall never forget the rich look of the countryside, especially at the eastward end of the island, around Taormina, in the fertile foothills of Mount Etna. Though Sicily dries up in the summer, it is greener than Ireland in the spring.

Mountains terraced to the top with almonds and olives, vines and beans. Miles of orange and lemon groves and orange flowers throwing their scent half a mile or more. Wheat full-grown already and broad beans ripe in the pods.

I shall never forget the flowers. Wild gladioli and asphodel and love-in-the-mist and crimson clover and giant snapdragons and a spiky yellow thing I decided was an amaryllis, but the locals told me was an onion.

I didn't feel quite the same about it after that.

11 November 1956

THEY TALK WITH TEARS IN THIS SHADOW CITY

Today I'd planned to write about the best-dressed women in Paris. Halfway to the airport I changed my mind and caught the next plane to Vienna. With the border sealed, this is as near as you can get to the tormented Hungary, where I think every woman's thoughts have flown.

VIENNA, SATURDAY

This week there's not much waltzing in Vienna. The north wind is knifing across the city.

The big parties are cancelled, and there's an occasional riot instead.

The women in the coffee shops talk with tears in their eyes as they stir the whipped cream into the hot chocolate.

Even the famous baroque architecture, which ought to look so splendid, seems sad and seedy in the rain.

People talk of one thing only: **HUNGARY.** The two nations so closely intertwined.

RUMOUR IS RIFE

The woman who wrapped up my parcel in a shop already has a refugee child in her home.

A man I met by the frontier had come from Linz, hoping to creep over and search for his sister and her family.

A girl I dined with was trying not to cry into her soup. Her parents are in Budapest. She got out herself a few years ago in the refrigerated compartment of a meat van.

Like Lisbon in the war, Vienna is now a crossroads for refugees and a seedbed for rumours. (The Austrians are convinced that the Russians have an eye on Vienna.)

I have spent many hours talking to refugees who poured out before the frontier was closed by Russian tanks. A few still manage to trickle through, including a circus troupe with three bears.

MOST BEAUTIFUL

The Hungarians must be one of the most beautiful races in the world. In spite of the exhaustion, and the dirt, the sordid clothes and crumpled headscarves, what riveted my eye were the high, wide cheekbones and the oval chins. These people are Magyars, not slab-faced Slavs.

I asked dozens of them in a refugee camp why they had left. This wasn't a panic flight from a battle. It was an escape from something which had tortured them for years.

'We left because we were so terribly poor.'

'We left because we loathed the Russians. We have had ten years of grinding work and great poverty.'

THEY DREAM

'I left because they shot my father four years ago and put my mother in prison.'

'We left because it was impossible to send the children to school. Even the little ones had to earn money. In a family of five, four must work to scrape a living.' This was an educated woman who spoke four languages. Her husband had stayed behind to fight.

'We left because every Hungarian dreams of being free.'

'We left because the Russians are animals.'

They lay crowded shoulder to shoulder in a barracks on piles of straw. But small luxuries were arriving every hour. The relief work has to be loving and quick. Some of the children had toys and there were mounds of apples from which they could help themselves.

Each day the camps diminish in size, as new homes are found for Hungarians all over Europe. Even while I was talking to one woman with two young children, an Austrian woman arrived, said she had room for three, would provide food, clothes and pocket money, and whisked the family away.

But the quickest nation to help has been the Swiss. They didn't stop to take names and make lists. They sent buses and carried off a thousand people.

I went one day to have a look at the border. I had to leave the car in a village and walk the last two miles. The road was flat, misty, desolate and rather spooky. After a mile of walking I caught up with a man walking in the ditch – a Hungarian-born Austrian who meant just to walk across the border and join in. A perfectly futile mission, but people here are frantic to wade in and help.

Don't ask me how I found out his plans, for I had no interpreter, but by exchanging documents, making signs and getting out a few words, it's remarkable how much you can explain.

At the frontier there was a Russian tank manoeuvring around, a machine gun rattling off, and a few men rushing out of the Customs house with tommy guns. Also, an American photographer taking pictures from a ditch. Later that day the Customs house fell to the Russian tanks.

All along the border the partisans are sniping away with pathetic weapons. Inside the border the battles are violent and real. But I am afraid the whole story is summed up by the sad little picture of the tommy gun and the tank.

The active and the spectator gardener.

Anne and Gardening

Anne didn't really start to write about gardening until some years after she left the *Sunday Express*. But it would be like sawing my mother in half, not to write about her addiction to flowers and the garden. She loved plants, each one a personal friend. She knew the provenance of every flower, from the date she had sowed the seed, to where she had obtained some treasured holiday cutting. Every plant had a tale to tell. Anne would often be seen just wandering slowly around her garden, looking, and I really mean *looking*. Just standing quietly studying a plant or admiring a particular set piece.

Her love of plants had begun when she was a child. Initially helping her mother manage the front garden at their house in Bayswater. The plants were obtained from a barrow which toured the streets on a Saturday. Holidays were often spent with her brother, John, in Berkshire, where the woods were filled with violets, primroses, Solomon's seal. Anne would walk the fields with a collecting tin for flowers, using the evening for pressing her finds between books and blotting paper. Mother told me she knew every wild flower on the south side of the Bath Road, and would mention areas were she had seen marsh violets or picked bunches of wild orchids on fields long gone to make way for development.

Anne would be the first to say that she was in no sense a garden designer. Cottage gardening was her passion, and although her plot evolved and changed, it was always at its best in the spring. Anne had planted clouds of silver and grey trees – whitebeam, cherries, dogwoods and willow-leaved pear, which shared the space with ancient apple trees. Primroses spread like weeds on the dry chalk soil, interspersed with speckles of blue *Anemone blanda*, while hellebores and euphorbias jostled with the lily-of-the-valley, Solomon's seal and pulmonarias. Of course, daffodils were grouped through a small orchard, and red tulips punctuated the flower beds. Her favourite roses scrambled up the trees and honeysuckle twisted around the front windows. It was an enchanted place.

The garden was proportionally larger than you would expect by just looking at the tiny cottage front on, but, not content, Anne purchased an extra piece of land that butted on to the back to increase it further. Although there was a front gate for guests, family parking was hidden around the back, so the walk from the car wound you down through the garden before you reached the house, which was a pleasure, not a chore. As a child I would run as fast as I dared down the steep slopes that bordered the cottage (this involved an abrupt stop to prevent crashing into the back door). Mother travelled light. A small, hard, old-fashioned suitcase barely filled, as spares of everything were kept *in situ*, so there was no tiresome lugging from the car.

Italian prisoners of war had been drafted in to dig out a sunk garden, which was one of the main architectural features. I am not sure how this came about, although I have read their presence was a common sight in rural areas after the war, as POWs considered to be 'low risk' were allowed out of the camps to earn 'proper' money. Farms needed men to help with the harvests, and apparently the italians in particular relished the opportunity to work on the land. I can only assume that Anne inveigled them away en route to their more pressing work in the fields.

The garden itself was created on an undulating plot, which made it more interesting, but it must have been a huge effort for the men to dig this section out by hand, as the topsoil in the area is limited and the chalk base hard and unyielding. They did a sterling job. Their work has been much admired and the area was used more than any other spot in the garden, as it housed the outdoor table and chairs, where many a meal al fresco was enjoyed.

I'm sure the irony would not have been lost on those digging. While to us 'al fresco' translates as 'in the open air', to an Italian the phrase means 'in the cold' – or 'in prison', which of course they were.

After the war flowers took over from vegetables once more, but there was still an area for peas, beans and salads. (This being the only way you could obtain a broad bean at the 'proper' size – small.)

Anne had been a keen tennis player in her youth, and we also had a grass court which gradually fell into disrepair, and eventually became the 'croquet lawn'. Lawn being rather an exaggerated term as it was awash with plantains and potholes created by the rabbits. Osbert loved a game of croquet but he was a terrible cheat, his familiarity with the weeds turned to tactical advantage.

In the Osbert years the garden became more formal. Two pairs of Irish yews were planted to create a rather grand walk-through. Statues arrived, to be placed inside topiary arches, and old wood steps were replaced with brick. Hostas appeared for the first time, and our wooden table turned slate. Osbert himself was more of a 'spectator gardener', but he was very vocal and enthusiastic about the garden and would follow Anne round: 'Oh, darling, I *do* congratulate you.' These words would cheer her along much more than if he had taken up a fork himself.

Although Anne was a keen pruner, she was hopeless at clearing up. Piles of foliage and twigs would just be left on the path for others to remove. My partner, Nick, has cheerfully acquired her habit, saying if it was all right for 'the head gardener', then it is good enough for him.

Thank you, Mother.

It took her marriage to Osbert to kick-start her career as a freelance gardening writer. While she was the provider the security that regular employment provided was essential to her. It also suited her temperament to be a permanent member of staff. At the same time, it was apparent to her that Fleet Street was starting to wane. In 1969 she wrote the following note: 'Sad working in a declining industry, especially when it's hari-kari, not a natural death. The feeble editors, sloppy standards, untrained writers, change for the sake of change, the reasons ill-disguised. Nothing is ever rewritten. Such a staff shortage that none of the young ones get trained or disciplined.' It was no wonder she had started to look around for a second career, a new field to explore and a subject that wasn't just semi-congenial but one she adored.

In 1968 *Queen* magazine, then under the editorship of Hugh Johnson, commissioned Anne to write a series of articles on gardening. Obviously she was not a trained horticulturist, but she was a gifted writer, and she turned her mind to the subject that had been her passion since childhood. Knowing that the 'how to' article was not her field, she concentrated on writing about the people behind their gardens. That was it. Her second career was up and running. 'I literally didn't know which were the best catalogues, growers, etc. But all the people you met were heavenly. People who wouldn't want to talk about any other subject, would pour it out about their gardens. A year later I had a large circle of new friends, and my knowledge of plants expanded every day. I read and read.'

Anne wrote nine gardening books in all, including, in 1973, the very successful *Sissinghurst: the Making of a Garden*.

In 1978 Anne was invited to become a member of the Council for the Royal Horticultural Society. She always maintained it was to boost their image, as they were, until she joined, all male. Back to square one. As in Fleet Street, Anne became the token female presence. Similarly, some years earlier she had been asked to do a stint on the Council for the Royal College of Art.

But she certainly wasn't asked just to become 'one of the boys'. She was never that. It was the intelligence and presence she brought to projects that recommended her to these then-male enclaves.

One of the treats that came with the RHS membership, was to be on their judging committees. This included, as well as their fortnightly shows, the grand Chelsea Flower Show. I have to say this provided a delicious kickback for me. Anne was sent passes for every hour of every day that Chelsea was staged, from the arrival of the first pot to the removal of the last. For four years Anne doled me out a pass for the press day. I worked out that the best moment to attend was over lunchtime, when the place would be absolutely deserted apart from the odd grower, panicking over a badly placed seedling. I could wander through the marquees or stare at the show gardens absolutely unattended. (Indeed, I could have run amok with a bottle of glyphosate and no one would have stopped me.) I usually stayed on to gawp at the Queen, and sometimes for a glass of champagne in the early evening. When Anne retired from her position, I didn't bother to go back. I had been much too spoilt by my solo visits, and jostling along with the crowds didn't have the same appeal.

When Mother was thinking about retirement, I assumed that she would want to stay in the cottage and sell her flat in London. Wrong. `Why on earth would you think that?' It was sadly true, the garden had become difficult to manage, her knees had let her down, and the whole process frustrated her. If she couldn't interact in a meaningful way with the garden, then it was better to let it go.

Anne wanted to stay in London – more precisely, in Chelsea. Where everything necessary to her life was in walking distance. The cinema, theatre, galleries, restaurants, shops, and me. Indeed, if you wanted to find Mother in her later years, really the best way was just to walk down the King's Road. It was uncanny the number of times I would bump into her. Foxtrot Oscar was a lunchtime favourite, their *eggs benedict* a lure. I often spotted her adding the requisite 3 grains of sugar to a coffee, breaking the walk to Peter Jones with a beady eye placed on the world from a pavement cafe, or she might be spied faffing around the butchers and bakers of Chelsea Green.

Instead of watching plants, she had chosen as she got older to watch people.

WRY NOTE

There is always some sourpuss on whom spring fails to work its magic. I heard these remarks last week.

'Spring always brings me out in spots.'
'My hair comes out in handfuls.'
'I dread the garden – the weeds are a whole month early.'
'The sun makes the house look filthy.'
'It's the worst time of year for vegetables.'
'It's the worst time of year for illness.'
'I was woken at 5 a.m. by the blasted birds.'

Anne and me in the garden
at Rose Cottage.

Anne in 1951 - the year I was born.

Anne and Religion

I can safely say that Anne did not have a spiritual bone in her body. She loved visiting ancient churches of any denomination, but had little time for the values behind their construction. Anne also enjoyed a service if the music was well played and the choir in tune. She was perfectly happy to discuss religion and was interested in faith and why some people had it.

Osbert was a genuine believer, High Church, like his best friend, John Betjeman. His faith was as much a part of his life as his love of old buildings or books and architecture. This is not to say he shone as a practising churchgoer. Midnight Mass at Christmas, Communion at Easter, and of course the usual rounds of weddings, funerals and memorial services. In his later years, when it was difficult to get him to church, then the church came to him. This involved Anne moving a heavy rosewood card table into a suitable position and locating a linen face towel (put aside for the purpose), before switching off the telephone and retiring to a safe distance in another room.

After the Communion, Mother would ask Osbert if he felt better, happier or more uplifted for his moment with God. 'Of course not,' he would say. 'You don't understand anything about it.'

'But is it a comfort to you?'

'Certainly not, that's not what it's for.'

'Then what is it for?'

'Not to make me feel better. Religion has nothing to do with comfort, the important thing is to *believe*.'

Well, he was quite right. She did not understand.

As for Catholicism, she thought it dire. Penitence, contrition, confession and all that guilt, were not for her. She had considered religion and found it wanting. I did attend a Church of England school, but this was the same as knowing how to hold a knife and fork, it was socially useful to know your way round a prayer book and be able to join in the hymns. I was certainly not supposed to put the knowledge into practice. The formal burial of pets was frowned on. When my daughter was small, she caught us conducting the burial of a beloved dog in the garden. My daughter wanted a prayer to send him on his way. Anne was incandescent. No loud raging, but brooding fury and some mumbled words. I have to say it rather spoiled the moment.

Anne had strong moral values, and I was brought up not to think about race, ethnicity, sexual orientation or class. The subjects weren't discussed, because Anne would not have seen the need. Tolerance and respect were considered a given, if for no other reason than politeness. To impart all of that without proselytizing is quite an achievement.

Anne discussed her own death quite regularly – for many years before it was remotely necessary. In this area as in all others she wanted the process to be trouble-free, and to that end the odd letter would arrive with a nugget of information about certain papers, or maybe a telephone number that I might need, so when her time came everything would be well ordered.

Her own relatives had died in early middle age, and she was always horrified that she kept on going. After reaching the age of seventy, she decided she had lived too long. Anne made a living will, and was under no circumstances to be resuscitated should the moment come. As each new year came round, she would always say, 'I really can't go on any longer can I?' And she meant it.

Anne was particularly insistent that no money should be wasted on the funeral. I am sure if we could have built a pyre at the bottom of our garden she would have been quite happy with that. She requested that her ashes be scattered in the garden of her cottage, but by the time she died her cottage had been sold, so that was no longer an option. Knowing her aversion to religion, we opted for a humanist funeral, which I have to say was handled in just the way she would have wanted. I was lucky. A few years earlier, Anne had been a guest on *Desert Island Discs*, so she had already made her own choice of music for her final atoll.

She passed away painlessly at ninety-six, while having a hip operation in Winchester hospital. Questioning until the very end. 'I've had the most intelligent chat I've had in weeks with the doctor about the hereafter . . . I'm not a bit worried. I feel like it's all happening to somebody else. Any news? Well, you'd better go now, dear. No point in coming for the next couple of days. I shan't be worth seeing. Do keep in touch . . .'

Anne then gave me two notes of instruction. One for if she came round from the operation, one if she didn't. It still surprises me that instead of remaining in the hospital I just left, as she had asked, and drove back to London. As I entered the house the phone rang, and of course it was the nurse asking me to come back immediately. Anne died before I returned, as usual on her own terms. I would like to have known the doctor's views on the hereafter. I should have asked.

I was so late for Anne's funeral I nearly missed it. There was not one accident on the road but several, so the journey was one solid traffic jam, with continual phone calls between the undertakers, my brother and me. Would I like the coffin returned to base? Should they go ahead with the service? How far away was I now? I thought of the irony. I, who am never late, who think through the ramifications of any journey, was going to completely miss my mother's funeral. I couldn't decide if she would think this very funny, or be berating me from the box. The one thing I did know was she wouldn't want to be shuffling up and down the A34. In the end Nick threw caution to the wind, and drove the last few miles on the hard shoulder. We made the service, the sun shone and nobody prosecuted us. So just maybe there *is* a God.

Anne and Bert Hardy: the old friends.

Anne and the Last Word

The conversation below was to be our last. Her 'view' was from a bed in Winchester hospital, the builders' scaffolding covering her window. I have included it here in full because it so very 'Anne'.

As is her writing, it is short, sharp and to the point. It includes all the facets of her personality in just a few paragraphs. Control, stoicism, honesty, irony, intelligence and still that competitive streak – even from her bed she was delighted she had managed to nab the last newspapers off the trolley.

She died a few hours later.

'Don't take the notebook, it has addresses I need in the back – tear it out.'

'I love it here. I've had the most intelligent chat I've had in weeks with the doctor about the hereafter.'

'The nurses are so kind. They do their work, and just chat around the bed, perfectly normally, not like in the home, where they never smile, you know.'

'I'm really looking forward to breakfast. Yesterday I had a nice soft roll – really fresh – not like those bits of toast you get in the home.'

'I'd just like to move in here, but the view's not lovely is it? And it won't get any better when they take that lot down.'

'You remind me of that Chekhov line – *The Cherry Orchard*, or was it *The Three Sisters*? – "You are all in black, are you in mourning for your life?" '

'The papers? Oh well, I just had to have them. I got the last from the trolley. Those dreadful M.Ps [referring to the expenses scandal]. I was once asked to sign a resident's parking permit for a friend who lived out of town and came to London a couple of times a month and wanted one. I refused. Other friends said they would have done it, but I just couldn't lie on a form. Would you have done it? She never liked me much afterwards.'

'I'm not a bit worried. I feel like it's all happening to someone else. Any news? Well, you'd better go now, dear. No point in coming for the next couple of days. They tell me I shall be in some pain, but they will be monitoring it. I shan't be worth seeing. Do keep in touch . . .'

Index

Acknowledgements

Author's acknowledgements

My thanks to Melanie Llewellyn from Getty Images for her enthusiasm and efficiency.

To Jo, Gail and Becky at Pimpernel for their unfailing good cheer, and glasses of wine.

To *Daily Express*/Express Syndication for allowing me to use Anne's articles – without which there would be no book.

To all the photographers past and present. Your images have given me great joy.

And finally to family life . . . who would we be without it . . .

Picture credits

The author and the publishers have made every effort to contact holders of copyright works. Any copyright holders we have been unable to reach are invited to contact the publishers so that full acknowledgement may be given in subsequent editions. For permission to reproduce the images on the pages listed below we would like to thank the following.

Cecil Beaton/*Vogue*/© Condé Nast Publications Ltd: page 26
© Bill Brandt/*Picture Post*/Hulton Archive/Getty Images: page 103
© Ernest Castro: page 152
© John Chillingworth/*Picture Post*/Hulton Archive/Getty images: page 153
© *Daily Express*/Hulton Archive/Getty Images: page 185
© Jillian Edelstein: page 205
© Felix Fonteyn: page 34
© John Gay: pages 82, 86, 150, 200
© Bert Hardy/*Picture Post*/Hulton Archive/Getty images: page 170 and front cover
© Macdonald Hastings: pages 46, 142
© Osbert Lancaster: pages 120, 178
© Felix Mann: page 39
© Jock Murray: page 106
© PA Images: page 96
© *Picture Post*/Hulton Archive/Getty images: pages 2, 14
Terence Spencer/ © Apple Corps Ltd: page 180